John Charles Frémont

and the Great Western Reconnaissance

General Editor

William H. Goetzmann
Jack S. Blanton, Sr., Chair in History
  University of Texas at Austin

Consulting Editor

Tom D. Crouch
Chairman, Department of Aeronautics
  National Air and Space Museum
  Smithsonian Institution

WORLD EXPLORERS

John Charles Frémont
and the Great Western Reconnaissance

Edward D. Harris

Introductory Essay by Michael Collins

CHELSEA HOUSE PUBLISHERS

New York · Philadelphia

Chelsea House Publishers
Editor-in-Chief   Nancy Toff
Executive Editor   Remmel T. Nunn
Managing Editor   Karyn Gullen Browne
Copy Chief   Juliann Barbato
Picture Editor   Adrian G. Allen
Art Director   Maria Epes
Manufacturing Manager   Gerald Levine

World Explorers
Senior Editor   Sean Dolan

Staff for JOHN CHARLES FRÉMONT AND THE
GREAT WESTERN RECONNAISSANCE
Deputy Copy Chief   Mark Rifkin
Editorial Assistant   Nate Eaton
Picture Researcher   Wendy Wills
Series Design   Loraine Machlin
Production Manager   Joe Romano
Production Coordinator   Marie Claire Cebrián

7   9   8   6

Library of Congress Cataloging-in-Publication Data

Harris, Edward D.
John Charles Frémont and the great Western reconnaissance/Edward D. Harris.
p.   cm.—(World Explorers)
Includes bibliographical references.
Summary: A biography of the nineteeth-century soldier, politician, and explorer whose many expeditions helped open up the western territories to settlers.
ISBN 0-7910-1312-X
1. Frémont, John Charles, 1813–1890—Juvenile literature.
2. Explorers—United States—Biography—Juvenile literature.
3. Soldiers—United States—Biography—Juvenile literature.
4. Presidential candidates—United States—Biography—Juvenile literature. [1. Frémont, John Charles, 1813–1890. 2. Explorers.] I. Title. II. Series.
E415.9.F8H27   1990
973.6'092—dc20   89-25180
[B]   CIP
[92]   AC

CONTENTS

WORLD EXPLORERS

THE EARLY EXPLORERS

Herodotus and the Explorers of the Classical Age
Marco Polo and the Medieval Explorers
The Viking Explorers

THE FIRST GREAT AGE OF DISCOVERY

Jacques Cartier, Samuel de Champlain, and the Explorers of Canada
Christopher Columbus and the First Voyages to the New World
From Coronado to Escalante: The Explorers of the Spanish Southwest
Hernando de Soto and the Explorers of the American South
Sir Francis Drake and the Struggle for an Ocean Empire
Vasco da Gama and the Portuguese Explorers
La Salle and the Explorers of the Mississippi
Ferdinand Magellan and the Discovery of the World Ocean
Pizarro, Orellana, and the Exploration of the Amazon
The Search for the Northwest Passage
Giovanni da Verrazano and the Explorers of the Atlantic Coast

THE SECOND GREAT AGE OF DISCOVERY

Roald Amundsen and the Quest for the South Pole
Daniel Boone and the Opening of the Ohio Country
Captain James Cook and the Explorers of the Pacific
The Explorers of Alaska
John Charles Frémont and the Great Western Reconnaissance
Alexander von Humboldt, Colossus of Exploration
Lewis and Clark and the Route to the Pacific
Alexander Mackenzie and the Explorers of Canada
Robert Peary and the Quest for the North Pole
Zebulon Pike and the Explorers of the American Southwest
John Wesley Powell and the Great Surveys of the American West
Jedediah Smith and the Mountain Men of the American West
Henry Stanley and the European Explorers of Africa
Lt. Charles Wilkes and the Great U.S. Exploring Expedition

THE THIRD GREAT AGE OF DISCOVERY

Apollo to the Moon
The Explorers of the Undersea World
The First Men in Space
The Mission to Mars and Beyond
Probing Deep Space

CHELSEA HOUSE PUBLISHERS

Into the Unknown

Michael Collins

It is difficult to define most eras in history with any precision, but not so the space age. On October 4, 1957, it burst on us with little warning when the Soviet Union launched *Sputnik,* a 184-pound cannonball that circled the globe once every 96 minutes. Less than 4 years later, the Soviets followed this first primitive satellite with the flight of Yury Gagarin, a 27-year-old fighter pilot who became the first human to orbit the earth. The Soviet Union's success prompted President John F. Kennedy to decide that the United States should "land a man on the moon and return him safely to earth" before the end of the 1960s. We now had not only a space age but a space race.

I was born in 1930, exactly the right time to allow me to participate in Project Apollo, as the U.S. lunar program came to be known. As a young man growing up, I often found myself too young to do the things I wanted—or suddenly too old, as if someone had turned a switch at midnight. But for Apollo, 1930 was the perfect year to be born, and I was very lucky. In 1966 I enjoyed circling the earth for three days, and in 1969 I flew to the moon and laughed at the sight of the tiny earth, which I could cover with my thumbnail.

How the early explorers would have loved the view from space! With one glance Christopher Columbus could have plotted his course and reassured his crew that the world was indeed round. In 90 minutes Magellan could have looked down at every port of call in the *Victoria's* three-year circumnavigation of the globe. Given a chance to map their route from orbit, Lewis and Clark could have told President Jefferson that there was no easy Northwest Passage but that a continent of exquisite diversity awaited their scrutiny.

In a physical sense, we have already gone to most places that we can. That is not to say that there are not new adventures awaiting us deep in the sea or on the red plains of Mars, but more important than reaching new places will be understanding those we have already visited. There are vital gaps in our understanding of how our planet works as an ecosystem and how our planet fits into the infinite order of the universe. The next great age may well be the age of assimilation, in which we use microscope and telescope to evaluate what we have discovered and put that knowledge to use. The adventure of being first to reach may be replaced by the satisfaction of being first to grasp. Surely that is a form of exploration as vital to our well-being, and perhaps even survival, as the distinction of being the first to explore a specific geographical area.

The explorers whose stories are told in the books of this series did not just sail perilous seas, scale rugged mountains, traverse blistering deserts, dive to the depths of the ocean, or land on the moon. Their voyages and expeditions were journeys of mind as much as of time and distance, through which they—and all of mankind—were able to reach a greater understanding of our universe. That challenge remains, for all of us. The imperative is to see, to understand, to develop knowledge that others can use, to help nurture this planet that sustains us all. Perhaps being born in 1975 will be as lucky for a new generation of explorer as being born in 1930 was for Neil Armstrong, Buzz Aldrin, and Mike Collins.

The Reader's Journey

William H. Goetzmann

This volume is one of a series that takes us with the great explorers of the ages on bold journeys over the oceans and the continents and into outer space. As we travel along with these imaginative and courageous journeyers, we share their adventures and their knowledge. We also get a glimpse of that mysterious and inextinguishable fire that burned in the breast of men such as Magellan and Columbus—the fire that has propelled all those throughout the ages who have been driven to leave behind family and friends for a voyage into the unknown.

No one has ever satisfactorily explained the urge to explore, the drive to go to the "back of beyond." It is certain that it has been present in man almost since he began walking erect and first ventured across the African savannas. Sparks from that same fire fueled the transoceanic explorers of the Ice Age, who led their people across the vast plain that formed a land bridge between Asia and North America, and the astronauts and scientists who determined that man must reach the moon.

Besides an element of adventure, all exploration involves an element of mystery. We must not confuse exploration with discovery. Exploration is a purposeful human activity—a search for something. Discovery may be the end result of that search; it may also be an accident, as when Columbus found a whole new world while searching for the Indies. Often, the explorer may not even realize the full significance of what he has discovered, as was the case with Columbus. Exploration, on the other hand, is the product of a cultural or individual curiosity; it is a unique process that has enabled mankind to know and understand the world's oceans, continents, and polar regions. It is at the heart of scientific thinking. One of its most significant aspects is that it teaches people to ask the right questions; by doing so, it forces us to reevaluate what we think we know and understand. Thus knowledge progresses, and we are driven constantly to a new awareness and appreciation of the universe in all its infinite variety.

The motivation for exploration is not always pure. In his fascination with the new, man often forgets that others have been there before him. For example, the popular notion of the discovery of America overlooks the complex Indian civilizations that had existed there for thousands of years before the arrival of Europeans. Man's desire for conquest, riches, and fame is often linked inextricably with his quest for the unknown, but a story that touches so closely on the human essence must of necessity treat war as well as peace, avarice with generosity, both pride and humility, frailty and greatness. The story of exploration is above all a story of humanity and of man's understanding of his place in the universe.

The WORLD EXPLORERS series has been divided into four sections. The first treats the explorers of the ancient world, the Viking explorers of the 9th through the 11th centuries, and Marco Polo and the medieval explorers. The rest of the series is divided into three great ages of exploration. The first is the era of Columbus and Magellan: the period spanning the 15th and 16th centuries, which saw the discovery and exploration of the New World and the world ocean. The second might be called the age of science and imperialism, the era made possible by the scientific advances of the 17th century, which witnessed the discovery of the world's last two undiscovered continents, Australia and Antarctica, the mapping of all the continents and oceans, and the establishment of colonies all over the world. The third great age refers to the most ambitious quests of the 20th century—the probing of space and of the ocean's depths.

As we reach out into the darkness of outer space and other galaxies, we come to better understand how our ancestors confronted *oecumene*, or the vast earthly unknown. We learn once again the meaning of an unknown 18th-century sea captain's advice to navigators:

> And if by chance you make a landfall on the shores of another sea in a far country inhabited by savages and barbarians, remember you this: the greatest danger and the surest hope lies not with fires and arrows but in the quicksilver hearts of men.

At its core, exploration is a series of moral dramas. But it is these dramas, involving new lands, new people, and exotic ecosystems of staggering beauty, that make the explorers' stories not only moral tales but also some of the greatest adventure stories ever recorded. They represent the process of learning in its most expansive and vivid forms. We see that real life, past and present, transcends even the adventures of the starship *Enterprise*.

The Making of a Hero

Early on the morning of August 15, 1842, a small band of climbers made its final assault upon a snowy peak in the Wind River range, in the west-central portion of what is now the state of Wyoming. The expedition's leader was Lieutenant John C. Frémont, a handsome, young American explorer commissioned by the Army Bureau of Topographical Engineers to survey and map the wilderness along the Platte and Kansas rivers. It had taken almost two months for the train of animals and men to inch its way across the Great Plains from its departure point, Chouteau's Landing, a trading post near the site of present-day Kansas City, Kansas. Food had been scarce at times, the weather unpredictable, and roving bands of Indians had threatened the journeyers' sense of security, if not their actual safety. By the time the expedition reached South Pass, a broad natural passageway through the Rocky Mountains, 950 miles from Chouteau's Landing, most of the men were eager to begin the journey back to civilization. They had accomplished what they had set out to do, and the success of their expedition would help make the Oregon Trail—the primary overland route used by pioneers and settlers to reach the Great Northwest—a safer way west, but their ambitious and mercurial leader was not satisfied. Frémont had set his sights on the Wind River Mountains, a range of the Rocky Mountains just to the

The Pathfinder, John Charles Frémont, from a daguerreotype taken by the American photographer Mathew Brady, who would earn his greatest fame for his photographs of the Civil War.

A romantic mid-19th-century rendering of Frémont's conquest of Frémont Peak. Immortalized in numerous images such as these, Frémont's mountaineering feat captured the imagination of the American people, who saw it as a symbol of the young republic's courage and vitality.

northwest of South Pass, and was determined to conquer what he believed to be its highest peak.

The lieutenant selected 5 men to accompany him on the ascent; the rest of the expedition, which totaled about 40 men in all, waited in the base camp below. While their trusty mules negotiated the slippery, rocky slopes, the mountaineers climbed slowly and carefully, trying to adjust to the high altitude, the effects of which had left their commander nauseous, light-headed, and irritable. In his uncharacteristic pique, Frémont had even dismissed the expedition's most valuable member, the legendary scout Kit Carson, from the select group that would attempt the summit. Within several hours, according to the report Frémont submitted to Congress later, they glimpsed the peak, some 3,000 feet above them atop a vertical granite wall. Far below, on the other side of their path, a vast chasm opened into a rich green valley where three mountain lakes sparkled like jewels. As the climbers approached the snow line, their route became steeper and more treacherous, forcing them to leave behind the mules and all unnecessary supplies.

The mountain's final obstacle was an imposing rock buttress that jutted out from a sheer precipice several hundred feet into the air. Frémont led the way, wedging his hands and feet into vertical crevices and maneuvering around the wall to the crest on the other side. Then, he vaulted onto the icy summit, nearly overshooting his mark and plunging into the abyss 500 feet below. Although he was only about five and a half feet tall, atop the peak Frémont cut a magnificent figure in his heavy overcoat, sash, and dashing silk scarf drawn neatly around his neck, the wintry wind tossing his wavy, brown hair about his shoulders.

As there was only room for one person at the top, each man took his turn, surveying all that lay below. The explorers commemorated their ascent by firing off pistols, sharing a glass of brandy, and raising a special American flag decorated with 13 stripes, 26 stars, and an eagle holding arrows and an Indian peace pipe in its claws. Frémont also made a rough estimate of the peak's altitude using a homemade barometer. His measurement of 13,570 feet above sea level only underestimated the height by 200 feet or so, but even with a more accurate reading the peak upon which the little band stood was not even the highest in the Wind River range, let alone the Rockies. But it is doubtful that even this knowledge would have tempered Frémont's joy. As the climbers savored this proud moment, a solitary bee landed on the knee of one of the men. In his report to Congress, Frémont portrayed the insect as a lonely pioneer of its species that had crossed the great mountainous divide to foretell the arrival of American civilization. The words could as well have pertained to himself, for Frémont's presence on this remote crag all but announced the United States's determination to reach boldly beyond its established boundaries and expand to the west. In the months to come, Frémont's published reports and other written accounts would capture the American imagination and immortalize the image—the brave, dashing young lieutenant, the advance scout of American civilization, planting the flag atop a previously unconquered peak—that would come to symbolize the young republic's determination to fulfill its manifest destiny by settling and "civilizing" the great tracts beyond the Mississippi River, lands theretofore thought of by many as the Great American Desert.

Among the cherished American ideals Frémont embodied was that of the self-made man. He was born out of wedlock on January 21, 1813, in Savannah, Georgia. His mother was Anne Pryor (née Whiting); his father, Jean Charles Frémon, a dashing, artistic Frenchman usually employed as a teacher of his native language. Frémon wooed Anne from her loveless 12-year marriage to Major John Pryor, a respected Virginia squire 45 years her senior, a union

Some of Frémont's men catch their first glimpse of the Wind River range. This illustration is from a mid-19th-century edition of one of Frémont's reports to Congress, which became best-sellers.

The specially designed American flag that Frémont carried with him to the top of Frémont Peak and later presented as a gift to his wife, Jessie.

she had agreed to at age 17 only in order to salvage her family's flagging fortunes. When Anne's love affair aroused the censure of her husband and Virginia society, she and Frémon ran off to Savannah, where she gave birth to John and his younger sister Anne. Several years of wandering ensued, during which Anne gave birth to two more children and the major died, freeing Frémon to marry his beloved. He did so, but early in 1818 he also fell ill and died. Anne Frémon then settled her family in Charleston, South Carolina. She was forced to take in boarders to support her family, but their relative poverty and his dubious pedigree seem not to have been a great obstacle for her oldest son to overcome, most likely because his obvious intelligence and ready charm endeared him to adults who could serve as his patrons. Always energetic and adventurous, young Charley, as he was called, made friends easily, and even as a young boy he had his father's striking looks: shoulder-length curly brown hair, penetrating light blue eyes, and smooth, dark skin.

A Charleston lawyer, John W. Mitchell, was the first in a series of influential older men who were to take a special interest in Frémon. (He added the *t* to his name sometime around 1836 in order to make it sound more American.) Mitchell employed the 14 year old as a clerk in his office, but the boy's ready grasp of complex concepts soon convinced Mitchell to pay his way through a prestigious local private school. There the youngster won the attention of Dr. Charles Robertson, who introduced him to classical languages and literature and encouraged him to develop his natural talent as a writer and a scientist. Frémont's abilities were so great that Robertson arranged for him to enroll at Charleston College when he was only 16. Although Frémont found college courses quite easy, he was equally attracted by activities such as sailing and pursuing young women, and after only a few months he was so behind in his work that he was asked to leave.

The next few years were spent teaching at a private school, where aside from his classroom responsibilities, Frémont read a tremendous amount on his own and developed his interest in astronomy, geology, and cartography. He also taught himself the basics of navigation and how to calculate latitude and longitude using scientific instruments. The chance to make practical use of his new knowledge came about as a result of his friendship with one of Charleston's first citizens, the well-traveled Joel Roberts Poinsett, who had just finished a stint as the United States's minister to Mexico. Poinsett's tales of the diplomatic service aroused his protégé's wanderlust, and Frémont jumped at the opportunity when Poinsett offered him a job as a math teacher aboard the warship *Natchez* during its tour of the coast of South America. (Before the U.S. Naval Academy was founded, it was common for sailors to receive their education from teachers on ship.) The *Natchez* was at sea for two years, until the spring of 1835. Frémont's first experience of exotic lands whetted his appetite for further adventure.

Frémont's early mentor and patron, Joel Roberts Poinsett. During his illustrious career, Poinsett served in the U.S. House of Representatives, as the first U.S. minister to Mexico, as secretary of war under President Martin Van Buren, and directed the second war against the Seminoles. Poinsett was an avid naturalist; the poinsettia plant, which he brought from Mexico, is named after him.

The chance to satisfy this hunger arose almost immediately. That same year, through Poinsett's influence, Frémont was selected to accompany Captain William G. Williams of the U.S. Topographical Corps on a survey to plan a railroad route from Charleston to Cincinnati. As an assistant engineer, Frémont was required to work long hours in difficult wilderness conditions, yet he found his labors exhilarating and described the job as "a kind of picnic with work enough to give it zest." In the fall of 1836, Frémont made another expedition with Williams, this time to survey the Cherokee territory near the intersection of the borders of North Carolina, Tennessee, and Georgia. At the time, the federal government was preparing to force the Cherokee from their ancestral lands in order to make room for white settlers. The purpose of the survey was to provide the government with more detailed information about the land in question so as to make the removal program easier to implement. Frémont never questioned the wisdom of the government's policy, which culminated in the infamous Trail of Tears, the forced migration west on which up to one-half of the Cherokee population perished, but he did recognize that he had found his calling. "Here I found the path which I was destined to walk," he wrote later. "Through many of the years to come the occupation of my prime life was to be among Indians and in waste places."

His heart set on further exploration of America's vast uncharted spaces, in late 1837 Frémont applied for a commission with the Army Bureau of Topographical Engineers. The soldiers of the bureau considered themselves the army's intellectual elite. Most were engineers and had graduated near the top of their class at West Point, but the appointment of Frémont's mentor Joel Poinsett to the position of secretary of war by President Martin Van Buren virtually assured that his application would receive respectful treatment. In April 1838, Frémont learned that he had been chosen as a civilian assistant on an expedition to survey the northern territory between the Mississippi and Missouri rivers. The expedition was an important one, and it represented a prime opportunity for Frémont. The land to be charted was part of the vast tract purchased by Thomas Jefferson from France in 1803. Although the Louisiana Purchase virtually doubled the territory of the United States, it had not been thoroughly explored since the famous journey of Meriwether Lewis and William Clark in 1804–6, and for much of its reaches the government lacked adequate information on topography, suitability of the land for farming, indigenous populations, best overland routes for settlers, and other pertinent matters. Heading the expedition was the renowned explorer and scientist Joseph Nicolas Nicollet.

Nicollet was a bit more polished than the rough-and-ready adventurers one expected to find in the West. A mathematician, astronomer, and former university professor, Nicollet had come to the United States from his native France in 1832 to fulfill his dream of exploring the West. By 1838, he had explored extensively in the Appalachian Mountains, been up the Red and Arkansas rivers, and charted the upper Mississippi, where he learned much about the Indian tribes residing there. When not in the wilderness, he enjoyed nothing more than talking theology and science over a good meal with the learned Jesuits of St. Louis, the river city that was the jumping-off point for most western expeditions. Frémont could not have found a better mentor in the serious business of scientific exploration. He was already well versed in the techniques necessary for survival in the wilderness, but it was Nicollet who would impress upon him that all his observations and measurements had to be precise if they were to possess scientific validity.

Frémont joined Nicollet in St. Louis in the spring of 1838 and was immediately placed in charge of provisioning the expedition. Pierre Chouteau, proprietor of the American Fur Company, assisted Frémont with this task, making sure nothing was left out. They brought with them plenty of food, including barreled pork, ham, bacon, dried and smoked beef, sugar, salt, flour, tea, coffee, bread, and butter. The long list of equipment featured rifles, ammunition, canoes, carts, lanterns, barometers, chronometers, microscopes, magnifiers, thermometers, compasses, pencils, paper, a sextant, medical supplies, matches, axes, pots, pans, knives, forks, spoons, soap, and rain gear. Each man was responsible for his own clothing, which typically consisted of buckskin shirts and trousers, wool socks, leather moccasins or sturdier boots, and a wide-brimmed, feather-laden hat. Thirty mules and horses were purchased to carry most of the supplies, although the men were also expected to shoulder some of the load. Frémont also made sure to pack some wilderness luxuries: wine, tobacco, claret, and cognac, as well as assorted metal products and Venetian glass beads to be used as gifts of goodwill to the Indians.

Of even greater importance was selecting the men for the expedition, which was Nicollet's responsibility. The

Fort Snelling overlooked the Minnesota and Mississippi rivers. At the time of Frémont's visit there with Joseph Nicollet, it was the most significant U.S. military installation in the West.

most experienced hands chosen were *voyageurs*, French fur trappers and hunters, descendants of the French pioneers who had settled the Mississippi Valley in the mid-17th century and had taken the lead in exploring the trans-Mississippi west. Many were *métis*, as those of mixed French and Indian blood were known. With their long hair and woolly beards, usually clad in buckskin and carrying a Hawken rifle (said to be able to fell a grizzly bear at 200 yards), the voyageurs looked intimidating, but they were highly regarded for their woodcraft and courage.

The expedition left St. Louis early in May 1838. The first leg of the journey was made by steamboat up the Mississippi River to Fort Snelling, an imposing structure 500 miles northwest of St. Louis at the confluence of the Mississippi and Minnesota rivers. After several days of rest and reprovisioning, the expedition set off overland to the west, following the course of the Minnesota River. The summer was spent surveying the land surrounding the Minnesota as far west as Lac qui Parle, near the present-day border of Minnesota and South Dakota. All the while, Nicollet and Frémont made careful written observations of the area's geology, plant life, soil composition, and topography, always with an eye toward the land's suitability for future settlement. At night, they took astronomical readings to chart the course of the rivers in the region. (The meticulous Nicollet himself took more than 90,000 instrument readings.) Frémont was most captivated by the qualities of the region known to the voyageurs as the Coteau des Prairies, the plateau that separates the Mississippi and the Missouri, and he wrote in a letter to a friend that there was no word in English that could do justice to the landscape's beauty.

The Sioux, Chippewa, and Cheyenne Indians the expedition encountered also made an impression on Frémont. The Indians were extremely helpful to the whites, especially when gifts were exchanged and food was shared

These Cheyenne Indians were photographed in their village on the Washita River, in present-day Oklahoma, in 1869. The Cheyenne that Frémont encountered still lived and hunted on their traditional lands; the tribe's forced relocation to Oklahoma took place several decades later.

between the two groups. The native people aided the American explorers in identifying and locating particular lakes, streams, and mountains, some of which had been named by Indians or early French explorers. Near the mouth of the Cottonwood River, the party was visited by a towering Sioux chieftain—in his *Memoirs of My Life*, published in 1887, Frémont said the Indian was seven feet tall—who warned them that they were about to pass into lands inhabited by hostile tribes. The Sioux's eloquent lamentation about the hard times that had befallen his tribe moved Frémont, who re-created it in a letter to Poinsett:

> Then, the buffalo covered the plains. Our enemies fled before us & the blaze of our fires was seen from afar, but they have dwindled away until their light is almost extinguished. There is no more game & my people are few & our enemies press us on every side. We thought that we were to die when the snow comes but you come & bring us life. [Nicollet had told the chief that the whites had come to bring food to the Indians.] Our sky was covered with clouds & dark with storm, but you came & again the sun shines bright in the blue heavens & we are happy.

On future expeditions, Frémont was usually respectful of the Indians, and he always made careful observations of their way of life. Like Nicollet, he usually attempted to negotiate a peaceful passage through Indian territory. To him, the Indians were as representative of his beloved wilderness—the "waste places," as he called it—as grizzly bears and untamed rivers. Yet despite his innate sympathy, the notion that the very purpose for which he was conducting his expeditions—to blaze a path for the expansion of white settlement—would most likely lead to the destruction of the Indians did not trouble him a great deal.

The exploring party returned to St. Louis in early December. A few weeks earlier, while still at Fort Snelling, Frémont learned that he had received a commission as a lieutenant in the Army Bureau of Topographical Engineers. From St. Louis, Nicollet and Frémont proceeded to Washington, D.C., where they presented a report of their findings to Lieutenant Colonel John James Abert, head of the bureau. The map Nicollet composed provided the most detailed picture to date of the upper Mississippi Valley. Pleased with their work (although not as enamored with Frémont's sloppy record-keeping), Abert quickly approved the young lieutenant's proposal for a "Military and Geographical Survey of the Country West of the Mississippi and North of the Missouri." Primarily, the new expedition would concern itself with the upper Missouri River, in what is now South Dakota and North Dakota.

The survey was again a success. After a steamboat ride of 1,000 miles upriver to Chouteau's outpost at Fort Pierre (most of the forts west of the Mississippi were not U.S. government installations but belonged to the fur companies that were most interested in exploiting the region), Nicollet, Frémont, and company explored as far north as Devil's Lake, with their greatest hindrance the region's bloodthirsty mosquitoes. The Sioux were again friendly. Although Frémont would proclaim in his memoirs nearly 50 years later that "here the Indians were sovereign," his mentor was aware that the days of their freedom were numbered. Nicollet's report on the expedition declared the upper Missouri region to possess great potential for white settlement once the Indians were removed.

When Frémont was not occupied with recording observations about the region's soil and climate, he often accompanied the métis on hunting trips on the plains. From the expedition's guide, Etienne Provost, a legendary mountain man who had trapped beaver in the Rocky Mountains as early as 1815 and claimed to have seen more of the West than any living white man, Frémont learned how to follow animal trails, how to kill buffalo in a large herd, and how to avoid getting lost in the wilderness. By journey's end, young Lieutenant Frémont had built a reputation as a skilled hunter and an inspirational leader.

Colonel John James Abert headed the Army Bureau of Topographical Engineers, the elite corps that conducted the most significant explorations of the West between 1838 and 1861. The bureau never numbered more than 36 officers.

The Flag Bearer

Frémont arrived in Washington, D.C., near the end of 1839 as a young man whose star was on the rise. Both of Nicollet's surveys had been deemed great successes, and his handsome and talented assistant was given his fair share of the credit. He was even asked to accompany his mentor on an official visit to President Van Buren as well as to dinners and receptions at many of the capital's finer houses. Most of Frémont's time, however, was spent at Nicollet's home, where the two men spent months organizing their data into an official report and constructing detailed maps. They were often visited by two men with a special interest in their work—Lieutenant Colonel Abert of the Army Bureau of Topographical Engineers and Thomas Hart Benton.

Benton was then approaching his 59th birthday and had served Missouri as its senator since its admittance as a state in 1821. Old Bullion, as Benton was known, was a committed opponent of the national bank and the expansion of slavery, but his favorite political issue was westward expansion. Although the term would not come into use until 1845, Benton was one of the earliest and most committed proponents of Manifest Destiny—the notion that the United States had the right and duty to expand its territory and influence throughout North America. He was most concerned with the lands between the Mississippi River and the Pacific Ocean and especially with the Oregon Country, which consisted of the present-day states of Washington and Idaho as well as Oregon. The Oregon

Frémont's dark good looks helped make him an American hero. In 1840, they also won him the heart of young Jessie Benton, the brilliant and beautiful daughter of his newest patron, Senator Thomas Hart Benton of Missouri.

region boasted much fertile farmland, abundant forests, and a profusion of fur-bearing animals. Its richness had led both Great Britain and the United States to covet it, and Benton was impatient for his country to act to solidify its claims there. The best method of doing so, Benton believed, was for Congress to grant land in Oregon to American settlers who were willing to make the dangerous overland trek to the Northwest. These pioneers would also have to be guaranteed the protection of the U.S. government, both in making their journey and once settled on their homesteads.

The United States's recent history seemed to confirm Benton's vision in that it had been a period of rapid westward expansion. Since 1815, the population of the region west of the Appalachians had grown more than twice as quickly as that of the original 13 colonies. Of the 13 states that had joined the original colonies, 11 lay west of the Appalachians. Others shared Benton's notion that the West represented America's future. "Eastward I go only by force, but westward I go free. Mankind progresses from East to West," wrote the sage of Walden Pond, the philosopher and writer Henry David Thoreau. For the hundreds of thousands of immigrants who would come to America's shores in the 1840s, the West represented freedom and the opportunity to own their own land. Once the effects of the economic depression that would last most of the decade began to be felt, thousands of longer-settled Americans also looked to make a new start beyond the Mississippi.

Not everyone agreed with Benton. Many Americans opposed a formal policy of westward expansion because they feared that it would aggravate the simmering conflict over slavery, as both sides of the issue were certain to be eager that their position prevail in the new territories. Others feared that American expansion would bring the United States into conflict and possibly even war with the other nations that had interests in the West—Great Britain and

The apostle of Manifest Destiny, Thomas Hart Benton, who wrote of the government's apparent indifference to the disposition of the Oregon Territory: "The title to the country thus being endangered by the acts of government, the saving of it devolved upon the people—and they saved it."

Mexico, which owned the southwest regions that would ultimately form the states of Arizona, New Mexico, Utah, Colorado, Nevada, and California. Even some of those who agreed with Benton's aims disagreed with his methods, which they believed amounted to a de facto annexation of the Oregon Country. They argued that a more prudent approach would be to negotiate with Britain and/or Mexico.

Benton believed that in order for Congress and the president to be convinced of the wisdom of his approach, more knowledge of the regions in question had to be obtained. Maps had to be drawn up, topographical, ethnographical, and climatic information compiled, routes charted. Most importantly, Americans had to be convinced the Oregon Territory could be safely reached and settled. Misconceptions about the geography of the West abounded. Some Americans believed that most of the western lands were barren waste ill suited to cultivation and human habitation, the Great American Desert that writer Washington Irving described in 1836 as "undulating and treeless plains, and desolate sandy wastes, wearisome to the eye from their extent and monotony." The fanciful notion that a great river flowed west from the Mississippi or Missouri, cut the Rockies, and flowed into the Pacific still held sway in some quarters.

Over the years, the U.S. government had not devoted a great deal of time and money to exploring the West. There had been the Lewis and Clark expedition, and in 1806 Zebulon M. Pike mapped a commercial trail to Santa Fe, but Pike's work was of greater use to traders than settlers and of little value for travelers to Oregon. In 1820, Major Stephen Long led a thorough and well-organized expedition to Colorado, but he did not go beyond the Rocky Mountains. The West's native inhabitants, the Indians, were of course intimately familiar with the trails, rivers, and mountains within their tribal territories, but Benton wanted professional surveys, prepared with an eye toward

Zebulon Pike, the lieutenant who traveled the headwaters of the Mississippi and was the first American explorer to cross what is today Colorado. Pike neither climbed nor named Pike's Peak, and he predicted that the sandy wastes along the Arkansas River would become the American Sahara, helping give rise to the myth of the Great American Desert.

(continued on page 30)

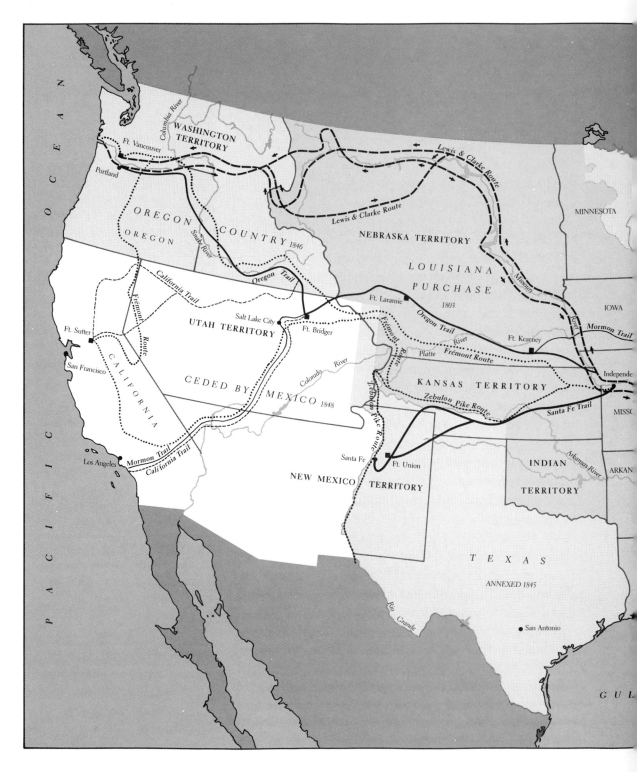

Westward expansion, 1803-1860

St. Lawrence River

Lake Superior

MICHIGAN

Lake Michigan

Lake Huron

MAINE

VT.

N.H.

WISCONSIN

NORTHWEST

Lake Ontario

NEW YORK

MASS.

Boston

CONN.   R.I.

Chicago

PENNSYLVANIA

New York

TERRITORY

OHIO

Philadelphia

N.J.

ILLINOIS   INDIANA

MARYLAND

DEL.

St. Louis

Ohio River

Washington

VIRGINIA

KENTUCKY

River

Nashville

NORTH CAROLINA

TENNESSEE

Memphis

SOUTH
CAROLINA

Mississippi

MISSISSIPPI   ALABAMA   GEORGIA

CEDED BY SPAIN

1819

New Orleans

FLORIDA

ATLANTIC OCEAN

OF   MEXICO

The United States and the
western lands at the time of
Frémont's first expedition. There
were then only three states west
of the Mississippi River—
Louisiana, Arkansas, and
Missouri.

(continued from page 27)

Major Stephen Long led an expedition in 1820 that reached as far west as the Rocky Mountains. The mission's military purpose was to establish a fort on the banks of the Yellowstone River, which proved impossible, but Samuel Seymour, a painter who accompanied Long, did become the first man to sketch the Rockies.

white settlement, and the government was not likely to rely on the assistance of people whose existence it preferred to forget. Hunters and trappers such as Jedediah Smith, Thomas "Broken Hand" Fitzpatrick, Kit Carson, and Jim Bridger had been roaming the West for decades. These mountain men each knew bits and pieces of western geography, but they never bothered to chart it accurately or create a comprehensive picture of the West. Although by 1840 representatives of the Rocky Mountain Fur Company had explored South Pass and the lands west, including a good portion of the Oregon Trail, Benton had in mind a comprehensive government-sponsored expedition, designed to convince Congress and the public of the benefits of westward expansion.

It did not take Benton and Frémont long to discover that they shared many of the same views on western exploration. The senator took the ambitious young lieutenant under his wing, and Frémont became a frequent visitor to the Benton family home. As Nicollet's health began to fail and it became apparent that he would never return to the wilderness, Benton began grooming Frémont to take Nicollet's place.

More than ambition and friendship attracted Frémont to the Benton household, for to the dismay of Old Bullion, it soon became apparent that his protégé and his vivacious daughter Jessie had fallen deeply in love. In 1840, when they met, Jessie was 15 years old, possessed of a striking figure and dark hair and eyes, but Frémont was equally taken by her "grasp of mind, comprehending with a tenacious memory; but with it a quickness of perception and instant realization of subjects and scenes in their complete extent . . . and a tenderness and sensibility that made feeling take the place of mind." Jessie was similarly smitten by the dashing young officer, whom she described as "slender, upright, elastic and tough as fine steel."

The romance incensed Jessie's parents. Frémont was Benton's choice to open the West, but he had more in mind for his daughter than a footloose army officer who intended to spend most of his life traipsing through rugged mountains and unknown canyons. Both Bentons also cited the age difference as grounds for their opposition, but this was apparently a smaller consideration for Jessie's mother, who had an idea of matching up her daughter with the president of the United States, Martin Van Buren, a widower 42 years older than the Bentons' dewy daughter. Believing that a wilderness trek might dampen Frémont's ardor, Benton dispatched him in the summer of 1841 to survey the land surrounding the lower Des Moines River in the Iowa Territory. The expedition lasted about six weeks. In his first opportunity at command, Frémont conducted himself with distinction, demonstrating that he was indeed Nicollet's logical successor. This gratified Benton nearly as much as the realization that the lieutenant had returned with his affection undiminished dismayed him.

One criticism that was never leveled at Frémont was that he was afraid to act. In the summer of 1841, with the Bentons forbidding the young lovers even to meet, Frémont and Jessie eloped and were married. However, no blissful but anxious honeymoon followed. After a ceremony at the home of a sympathetic friend, Senator John Crittenden of Kentucky, both returned to their own homes. It was more than a month before the couple mustered the courage to inform the Bentons. The news was enough to provoke a towering rage on the part of Old Bullion, who ordered Frémont from his house, adding that his daughter would stay with him. Jessie responded by saying that she intended to follow her husband, and when she offered a biblical quotation as demonstration of where her duty lay, her father realized the extent of her determination. He finally gave his grudging acceptance of the union but told the couple they would have to make their home with him and the rest of the family, to which they agreed.

In 1842, according to Benton, "upwards of a thousand

Jessie Benton eloped with John Frémont in the summer of 1841. Throughout their 49-year marriage, her loyalty and devotion to her husband knew no limits. Jessie was an accomplished writer; some have charged that her contributions to her husband's manuscripts were much greater than she has been given credit for.

Charles Preuss, the cartographer who accompanied Frémont on three of his expeditions. Preuss' precise maps and drawings lent scientific validity to Frémont's work; his mordant diary entries provide an interesting counterpoint to Frémont's glamorous narratives of his explorations.

American emigrants went to the [Oregon] country, making their long pilgrimage overland from the frontiers of the Missouri." Benton continued to press for land grants and guarantees of government protection, but Congress and President John Tyler were reluctant to rile the British. But Congress did grant the Army Bureau of Topographical Engineers its annual operating funds, and Benton convinced Abert to put $30,000 of that money to use for a western expedition to be headed by his son-in-law. Although the exact official purpose of the mission is still open to question, Frémont asserted in his memoirs that he convinced Abert to make South Pass the expedition's goal and that it was at least tacitly understood that one of the mission's raisons d'être was to encourage emigration to Oregon.

After a sorrowful parting from his three-months-pregnant wife, Frémont traveled to St. Louis in early May 1842. He spent the rest of that month in the bustling river city gathering supplies, assisted by the ever helpful Pierre Chouteau, and recruiting the 23 rugged adventurers who would accompany him. Nineteen of these were seasoned voyageurs who were well familiar with the wilderness life and were willing to endure several months of hardship for an average salary of 75 cents a day.

One of the expedition's most noteworthy members was Charles Preuss, a tall, ruddy-faced, grouchy German cartographer whom Frémont had befriended in Washington at a time when Preuss was down on his luck. Preuss, who would accompany Frémont on his second and fourth expeditions as well, was a well-respected scientist whose precise work on the expedition lent an air of authority to Frémont's published findings. In addition to his mapmaking, Preuss also collected samples of indigenous plant and animal life and made a number of valuable landscape sketches. The maps and drawings would help inform potential emigrants about what to expect in the western lands.

As the expedition's guide, Frémont hired on the legendary mountain man and scout Christopher "Kit" Carson, whom he met in early June aboard the steamboat that carried the expedition from St. Louis to Westport, the site of Chouteau's Landing and the expedition's jumping-off place. Modest, soft spoken, direct, somewhat short and on the slight side, Carson nonetheless had a commanding presence, owing at least in part to his confident blue eyes. Raised on the Missouri frontier, the illiterate Carson had learned his craft from the most celebrated American mountain men: the Sublettes, Jim Bridger, Joseph Walker, and Tom Fitzpatrick. Frémont would later portray Carson to the American public as a navigator with a near mystical sense of direction; grateful for the recognition he received for his work with Frémont, Carson would later declare that he owed more to him "than to any other man alive." Carson's value to the expedition was reflected in the princely salary Frémont agreed to pay him—$100 a month.

The company set out from Westport across the prairies on Friday, June 10. They traveled only a few hours on the first day in order to give themselves ample time to get accustomed to setting up camp and preparing for the next

Westport (present-day Kansas City, Kansas) was the jumping-off point not only for Frémont's early expeditions but also for emigrants heading west on the Oregon Trail.

day's journey. On a typical day, the men awoke at 4:30
A.M. and had a breakfast of biscuits and coffee while their
horses and mules grazed nearby. By 6:30, the sun was
coming up and the expedition was packed up and on its
way. They generally stopped at noon for an hour to relax
and have a bite to eat. The regimen included precautions
against attacks by Indians. Although most of the Indians
Frémont encountered were peaceful and even quite helpful, the explorers could not afford to take chances in a
land that was unfamiliar to them. When the caravan
stopped a little bit before sunset each day, the men arranged their wagons in a tight circle and set up camp inside
it. Campfires were built and supper prepared while the
animals were picketed and allowed to feed on what grass
and plants they could find in the area. As darkness fell,
the fires were extinguished to conceal the camp more
effectively. By nine o'clock, nearly everyone was asleep
inside their tents, although the men took turns standing
guard throughout the night.

On a good day, the expedition covered 25 to 30 miles,
depending on weather conditions and the terrain. At times,
the relentless summer heat slowed their progress and
caused illness and fatigue among the men. In stormy
weather, the animals moved more slowly and the wagons
often got stuck in the mud. The most difficult aspect of
daily travel was fording rivers. The water was usually deep,
very cold, and ran with a strong current, and swimming
was an outdoor skill that most voyageurs had not mastered.
When the travelers attempted to cross the swollen Kansas
River only a few days into the journey, they lost their
entire supply of sugar and coffee when an inflatable rubber
raft capsized. The prospect of making their way west without coffee greatly dismayed the voyageurs.

There were days at a time when travel across the empty
prairies was dreary and uneventful. Frémont occupied
himself by enforcing discipline among his men and doing
his best to keep morale high. Using the expedition's tele-

scope, he made careful astronomical notations twice a day and periodically determined the party's latitude and longitude with a sextant and a chronometer. He also kept a detailed journal of daily events and collected specimens of local plants and minerals. Preuss was placed in charge of plotting the expedition's progress on a map and sketching important landmarks along the route.

With Kit Carson directing the way, the expedition followed the faint outlines of the Oregon Trail along the Platte River through present-day Nebraska. When they reached the fork in the Platte, Frémont led a small group along the southern fork toward St. Vrain's Fort while Carson and the rest of the party followed the North Platte to Fort Laramie. Frémont split the expedition because he wanted to survey the uncharted southern region for favorable sites for the establishment of a line of outposts to connect the United States with the Rocky Mountains. On July 9, the overcast sky cleared enough to give Frémont's band their first glimpse of Long's Peak, a snow-covered crag at the eastern perimeter of the Rocky Mountains. The

Emigrants stream westward along the Oregon Trail near the Sweetwater River. The cleft in the granite ridge was known as Devil's Gate. On his first expedition, Frémont tried unsuccessfully to photograph this landmark, but he was not to succeed at obtaining daguerreotypes of the West until he brought a professional with him on his final expedition.

sight of the legendary range inspired the men with renewed vigor.

On the next day, they reached St. Vrain's Fort, located on the south bank of the South Platte, near the present town of Evans, Colorado. Their host was the cordial Marcellin St. Vrain, the fur trader and entrepreneur whose company operated the fort, which doubled as a trading post. After a rest of a day or so, they began the long march north to rejoin the remainder of the expedition. It took them 5 days to cover the approximately 110 miles to Fort Laramie, in what is now southeastern Wyoming, the best known of the American Fur Company's western outposts. The massive adobe structure had been built to provide maximum protection from without and relative comfort within. There were large square bastions on two of the four corners, each equipped with perches for riflemen. The living quarters faced onto the 130-foot-square courtyard. Frémont was especially impressed by the fort's "very cool and clean appearance," no doubt a refreshing change from the hot, dusty trail. While there, Frémont purchased a tepee from some local Indians; it would serve as his home on the trail during all his expeditions.

But at Fort Laramie, Frémont received disturbing news. While traveling the North Platte, Carson had encountered

Independence Rock was a major landmark along the Oregon Trail. In early years it had been the site for the annual rendezvous of the mountain men, a summer get-together during which trappers and hunters spent several weeks drinking, gambling, swapping stories, and trading furs with the local Indians.

his old wilderness buddy, the storied mountain man Jim Bridger. In his 25 years in the mountains, Old Gabe, as he was known, had endured all manner of hardship, but now he advised Carson that it would be impossible for the expedition to reach its proposed goal of the South Pass. Bridger had just returned from that area, and he had learned that Sioux warriors had ambushed several groups of emigrants bound for Oregon. It was said that the Sioux had formed an alliance with the Cheyenne and the Gros Ventre for the purpose of attacking the increasing numbers of settlers who were passing through their land. Once apprised of the danger, Frémont remained undaunted and announced that they would press on, but even as stalwart a hand as Carson was so worried that he made out his last will and testament before the expedition set off once more.

On the morning of July 21 the small party rode out from the shadow of Fort Laramie and headed west along the divide between the Laramie and North Platte rivers. They had no trouble with the Indians, although they did succeed in capturing two Sioux, who were set free after questioning revealed that they intended no harm to the whites. There were other encounters with Sioux, Arapaho, and Cheyenne warriors, many of them unhealthily thin, who told Frémont's interpreter, Joseph Bissonette, a fur trader who had had many Indian wives, that the land ahead had been ravaged by locusts and was unable to support human life. In early August the party reached Independence Rock, a massive granite boulder along the Sweetwater River, 650 yards long, 40 feet high, bare except for a lone dwarf pine tree on top and the names of the mountain men who over the years had carved their name in it, including those who had met there and held an uproarious Fourth of July party in 1825. Onward they pressed into the Rockies, seeing no evidence of the blight the Indians had described. On August 8, Carson at last guided the tired crew through South Pass, a wide, flat opening some 8,000 feet above sea level at the southern end of the Wind

Mountain man Jim Bridger in the 1860s. Bridger's tales of wilderness life often struck incredulous city folk as too fantastic to be true. "They said I was the damndest liar ever lived. That's what a mountain man gets for telling the truth," lamented Bridger. In later years, the illiterate Bridger traded a yoke of cattle for an edition of Shakespeare and paid a local youth $40 a month to read it to him. He became fond of declaiming the immortal Bard's work, often seasoning the poetry with creative oaths.

Mountain man Kit Carson first met Frémont on a steamboat in the summer of 1842. Of that meeting, Carson recalled later: "I told Colonel Frémont that I had been some time in the mountains, and thought I could guide him to any point he would wish to go." Carson's abilities more than made up for his lack of education; during the Civil War he was the only brigadier general in the U.S. Army who could neither read nor write. In later life he learned to read and even authored an autobiography.

River chain. Envisioning something more dramatic, both Frémont and Preuss found the pass uninspiring.

Frémont's ascent of the eponymous peak to the north more than assuaged his disappointment. After his report of the expedition was published, the conquest of Frémont Peak became immortalized as the very apotheosis of the spirit of manifest destiny, but one member of the expedition viewed the mountaineering and much of the entire journey more cynically.

Charles Preuss portrayed the great adventure with resounding distaste. According to the journal kept by the dour Preuss, the food on the expedition was terrible, the nights sleeping on hard ground were unpleasant, the prairie was tedious, and his companions were uncivilized rabble. He was also disappointed by the Rockies, which did not measure up to the magnificent Alps, and he found the climb to Frémont Peak most unpleasant: "No supper, no breakfast, little or no sleep—who can enjoy climbing a mountain under these circumstances?" His account of the ascent was noticeably free of the high drama with which Frémont colored it. Preuss charged that Carson exaggerated the danger of the Indian attack "in order to make himself important," and he criticized Frémont for being a "childishly passionate man."

Once Frémont's Peak was conquered, the expedition headed toward home, but several weeks of travail still lay ahead. The trip's greatest tragedy occurred at the end of August when Frémont, accompanied by several others, including Preuss, impetuously decided to shoot the rapids of the swift Sweetwater River in the rubber raft, which was laden with scientific equipment, Frémont's notes, and the specimens he had collected. The vulnerable craft picked up speed as it shot through the channel between high cliffs on either side. Emboldened and excited by their success, the voyageurs locked arms and broke into a verse from a Canadian boating song. When they reached the chorus, the boat ran head-on into a submerged rock and overturned. Much of the cargo was lost, including some of Frémont's journals, and the boat had to be abandoned.

The disaster dissuaded Frémont from taking any additional risks, and by October 1 the party had reached the farms near the confluence of the Platte and Missouri rivers that then represented the farthest reaches of American civilization. When Frémont arrived in Washington, D.C., at the end of October, he presented Jessie with the faded American flag he had taken to Frémont Peak. As he spread it out across her bed, he declared: "This flag was raised over the highest peak of the Rocky Mountains; I have brought it to you."

Frémont devoted the next several months to the painstaking task of shaping the data from the expedition into the coherent report he was expected to present to Congress. His days were brightened by the birth of his daughter Elizabeth, but he had a great deal of difficulty setting himself to the task of writing. After several false starts, he obtained better results by dictating his thoughts to Jessie, and on March 2, 1843, *A Report of an Exploration of the Country Lying Between the Missouri River and the Rocky Mountains on the Line of the Kansas and Great Platte Rivers* was presented to Congress. The 207-page report, which consisted of Frémont's high-spirited narrative, astronomical observations, latitude and longitude readings of key locations, a detailed map of the region between Fort Laramie and the Wind River range, and a catalog of plant and rock specimens, was hailed by the expansionists. Although the report contained little of lasting scientific value and was sloppy in many of its details, its buoyant tone convinced Congress to order 1,000 copies printed for sale to the public. All of them were quickly snapped up. Frémont was hailed as a hero, and preparations were quickly begun for a new expedition. This time the goal would be Fort Vancouver, the Hudson's Bay Company outpost deep within the Oregon Territory on the shores of the Columbia River.

Frémont and Carson carved their names in this rock in Jefferson County, Missouri, on their way west in 1842. It was common for mountain men, explorers, and settlers to leave some mark of their presence along the trail.

Onward to Oregon

Frémont's orders for his second expedition called for him to take a slightly southern route from Westport, along the Kansas and Republican rivers and then across the South Platte to the Sweetwater River and through South Pass. He would then cross the Rockies and make his way northwest to the Snake and Columbia rivers and ultimately to Fort Vancouver. The return trip was to be made via the Oregon Trail. Frémont's surveying and topographical work in the Northwest was intended to complement the findings of an earlier survey, the 1841 study of the Pacific Coast region conducted by Lieutenant Charles Wilkes of the U.S. Navy. Wilkes's report on his expedition, which also took him across the Pacific and to Antarctica, filled 16 volumes, and he returned with so many plant and animal specimens that the Smithsonian Institution was created to house them.

At St. Louis, Frémont again had no trouble recruiting voyageurs for the journey. Several had traveled with Frémont or Nicollet before, including Basil Lajeunesse, one of the most steadfast members of the first Frémont expedition. Even the irascible Preuss was willing to brave the wilderness again. With Carson off in the wild somewhere, having left Frémont at the conclusion of the earlier journey with the vague assurance that he would hook up with him on the trail should Frémont succeed in mounting a second expedition, Frémont hired as guide Thomas "Broken Hand" Fitzpatrick, a rugged 44-year-old mountain man whose hair had turned snowy white during an epic three-

The Pathfinder and his guide: Frémont (seated) and Carson.

day battle with Indians in the Wind River Mountains several years earlier. Fitzpatrick was the second-highest-paid member of the expedition, behind Preuss.

No one knows exactly what was on Frémont's mind at the outset of the journey, but in buying supplies he concentrated as much on weaponry as on scientific equipment. He personally selected for purchase 33 Hall's carbine rifles and 5 kegs of gunpowder. Although he had not been authorized to do so, he also managed to convince an army captain, Stephen Kearny, to supply him with a 12-pound mountain howitzer complete with carriage wagon and 500 pounds of ammunition. When Colonel Abert, alerted by Frémont's going far over budget, learned that he had also requisitioned a cannon, he sought to delay the expedition's departure, but by that time the 40-man party had set off for Westport, and in early June 1843 it moved out onto the Great Plains, far beyond the influence of the irate Abert.

Lieutenant Charles Wilkes commanded the U.S. Exploring Expedition of 1838–42, which circumnavigated the globe. Arrogant and aloof, Wilkes had attained the rank of admiral and had been court-martialed twice by the time this photograph was taken. Frémont's second expedition was supposed to complete the surveying work in the Pacific Northwest that Wilkes had begun.

At first, the group moved slowly, in part because Frémont had allowed some greenhorns, including a Harvard University law student, to hire on and he did not wish to tax them unduly at the outset. The rich grassland along the Kansas and Republican rivers, with its abundance of game and wildflowers, also gave reason to tarry. At times thousands of buffalo filled the prairies. The great shaggy beasts later gave Frémont the only chance he would find to use the howitzer, which, it had already become apparent to the men, was of absolutely no practical purpose. Undeterred by Preuss' grousing—"If we had only left that ridiculous thing at home," the cartographer wrote in his journal—Frémont conducted artillery practice on the passing herds, a murderous pastime Preuss characterized as "a cruel but amusing sport."

Between the Republican and the South Platte, the land turned barren. Streams slowed to a trickle, and dusty-looking sagebrush took the place of the wild roses and buttercups that had bloomed on the grasslands. Annoyed at their slow progress, by this point Frémont had split the expedition in two, taking command of the smaller and more mobile group and leaving Fitzpatrick in charge of the rest of the men and the provisions. He led his hungry band into St. Vrain's Fort on July 4, only to discover that the outpost was undersupplied and unable to provide his men with provisions or new animals.

In search of supplies and fresh pack animals, they then pressed on to Pueblo, a settlement about 100 miles due south of St. Vrain's Fort. The trip would have been for naught except for the timely arrival of Kit Carson, who volunteered to ride to Bent's Fort, a formidable adobe structure some 40 miles east along the Arkansas River, for the needed goods while Frémont and his men returned to St. Vrain's.

The reunited party (Fitzpatrick and his men having long since arrived) left St. Vrain's Fort on July 26. Nearly three weeks' travel took them across the South Platte and, in

Mountain man Thomas "Broken Hand" Fitzpatrick helped guide Frémont's second expedition west. Fitzpatrick later served as the U.S. government's first Indian agent in Colorado.

St. Vrain's Fort, an adobe structure on the South Platte River, was operated by William Bent and the brothers Ceran and Marcellin St. Vrain, partners in the fur-trading concern of Bent, St. Vrain & Company.

two separate groups again, through South Pass to the lush Green River valley, a popular site for the annual rendezvous of the mountain men in years past. Along the way the men were able to kill deer, buffalo, and antelope for meat, and there were several harrowing encounters with Arapaho, Cheyenne, and Sioux braves, although a tenuous peace was maintained.

Following the Oregon Trail west, Frémont and his band soon entered the Bear River valley. (The second group, headed by Fitzpatrick, had been sent ahead on the Oregon Trail to Fort Hall, located on the Snake River in present-day Idaho.) Frémont intended to join them there after making a detour south. By following the Bear River, his guides had told him, he would reach the Great Salt Lake, which for years had been the object of mystery and speculation. It was believed that in 1824 Etienne Provost had been the first white man to reach it, and it was known that a year later Jim Bridger had stood on its shores, convinced that he was gazing out over the vast expanse of the Pacific Ocean. Legend had it that somewhere on the lake's surface an enormous and powerful whirlpool raged endlessly and connected with the ocean through an underground river. Frémont was eager to see the lake for himself and to be the first to measure and survey it with scientific instruments.

On September 6, from the top of a butte they named Little Mountain, Frémont and six other men looked upon the Great Salt Lake for the first time. The magnificent waters stretched out beyond their vision "in solitary and still grandeur," in Frémont's words. He described the moment as "one of the great points of the exploration . . . as we looked eagerly over the lake in the first emotions of excited pleasure, I am doubtful if the followers of Balboa felt more enthusiasm when, from the heights of the Andes, they saw for the first time the great Western ocean."

The party spent the next several days exploring the lake and its islands in a rubber raft, although it was a somewhat dispirited group Frémont presided over. The presence of this seemingly endless body of salt water amidst the barren, rocky land of what Frémont would term the Great Basin struck his companions as unnatural. The absence of game animals also contributed to the low morale of the group, who were forced to eat sea gulls and roots and grasses to

The spectacular Green River valley in eastern Utah. Frémont visited the valley several times.

keep up their strength. For all his grumbling, Preuss possessed tremendous stamina, and he was able to make a fairly detailed and surprisingly accurate sketch of the lake.

The 100-mile journey north to Fort Hall took about a week, through land sparse with vegetation or game animals. At Fort Hall, the two parties were reunited, but the steady stream of travelers along the Oregon Trail had left the fort short of supplies, and its commander, Richard Grant of the Hudson's Bay Company, was able to sell Frémont only a few horses, which were in such poor shape that they were hardly adequate replacements for the expedition's weary mounts. While waiting out an ice storm at the fort, Frémont noted that the site would be an excellent one for a U.S. military outpost to protect wayfarers on the Oregon Trail. Another member of the expedition, 18-year-old Theodore Talbot, occupied himself recording his admiration for the Shoshoni Indians who came to the fort to trade. Talbot was particularly taken by their antelope- and deerskin shirts, their fringed leggings, their ceremonial robes of ermine or weasel fur, and their buffalo-hide shields.

Most of the rest of the men of the expedition were less sanguine about their plight, particularly when they learned that Frémont intended to press on to Oregon despite the lack of supplies. Most were hungry and tired and longed for home. When Frémont stated that he would pay off those who wished to return, 11 men took him up on the offer, including the redoubtable Lajeunesse. Surprisingly, Preuss opted to continue onward.

From Fort Hall the diminished party pushed on along the Snake River, through a monotonous landscape of sagebrush and lava boulders that Frémont characterized later as a "melancholy and strange-looking country—one of fracture, and violence, and fire." The ice storm proved to be an accurate harbinger of winter's early onset, as nighttime temperatures dipped below freezing. The food shortage was eased somewhat, however, in part because the

A herd of buffalo drink from the Platte River. A typical buffalo stands 5 feet tall at the shoulder and weighs 2,500 pounds. In the 1840s vast herds of buffalo still roamed the American prairies.

smaller band of explorers was easier to provide for, but
mostly because the friendly Shoshoni, who were adept at
spearing salmon from the Snake, proved willing to trade
with the whites.

In early October the party stopped briefly at Fort Boise,
where they were able to obtain some butter, then moved
on. From the rugged high country beyond the Snake Frémont gazed upon the mountain ranges to the south and
west and dubbed the desert region between the Rockies
and the western ranges the Great Basin. By the end of the
month, Frémont's band had crossed over the heavily
wooded Blue Mountains and reached a missionary settlement near present-day Walla Walla, Washington, where
the men were annoyed to learn that potatoes were the only
food item that could be purchased. Several days' hike along
the sandy shores of the Walla Walla River later, they at
last reached the mighty Columbia River, in Frémont's
words, "the great river on which the course of events for
the last half century has been directing attention and con-
ferring historical fame. The river is, indeed, a noble object,
and has here attained its full magnitude." Fed by the Snake
and Walla Walla, the Columbia at this point was 1,200
yards wide. Although the prospect of floating downstream
on the swift Columbia current no doubt appealed to the
thrill seeker in Frémont, he prudently allowed the tales of
the legendary Dalles—the series of massive waterfalls and
rapids past the mouth of the Deschutes River where the
Columbia squeezes between high cliffs—that he had heard
at the mission to deter him, much to the chagrin of the
ever-disagreeable Preuss.

The cartographer had much cause to grumble as the
small band spent the next several days slogging through
deep, loose sand along the Columbia. Not even the distant
silhouettes of Mount Saint Helens and Mount Hood could
relieve the drab monotony of the landscape. There were
so few trees that it was difficult to obtain wood to build
fires over which the unvarying diet of potatoes could be

*Two Shoshoni chiefs. The
Shoshoni were helpful to the men
of Frémont's expedition. They
had a tradition of aiding whites;
Sacagawea, the Indian woman
who guided the Lewis and Clark
expedition, was a Shoshoni.*

Indians were able to live in the rough terrain along the Columbia River near the Dalles, but the weary men of Frémont's party found the landscape depressing.

prepared, and in the mornings thin layers of ice often covered the streams that they crossed. Frémont found even the human inhabitants of this region to be unappealing. He called them "half-naked savages" and wrote later that "in comparison with the Indians of the Rocky Mountains and the great eastern plain, these are disagreeably dirty in their habits. Their huts were crowded with half-naked women and children, and the atmosphere within [was] anything but pleasant to persons who had just been riding in the fresh morning air." Once the Shoshoni Indian boy that Frémont had hired as a guide at Walla Walla took them inland south of the Columbia, the terrain became more pleasing. Frémont concluded that the wooded hills and valleys seemed to be well suited for settlement. Past the Dalles, Preuss got his wish, for Frémont bought a large cedar canoe, about 30 feet long, from a family of Wasco Indians. He also hired three of the Indians as boatmen. The Columbia's powerful current carried Frémont and 3 others of his party swiftly downriver, and within 2 days they were at Fort Vancouver, the great Hudson's Bay Company stockade, 700 feet long by 300 feet wide, at the site of present-day Vancouver, Washington. (The Hudson's Bay Company was a British corporation that had been granted a monopoly by the Crown on North America's fur trade. Its renowned trappers and traders plied the northern expanses of the continent from the Atlantic to the Pacific.) Frémont pronounced his weary band "a motley group, but all happy"; he misread the mood of the splenetic Preuss, however, who wrote of the river trip, "Never have I experienced such a disagreeable journey on water." Preuss' ire was no doubt aggravated by Frémont's request that he shave his beard and otherwise clean himself up before meeting the distinguished commander of the fort, John McLoughlin, a physician by training who had built a reputation for himself as one of the Hudson's Bay Company's most able traders. Preuss' refusal of Frémont's request led to a furious row between the two men.

The courtly McLoughlin managed to overlook Preuss' unkempt appearance. He greeted Frémont warmly and provided him with all the supplies that he would need for his return journey, despite his recognition that the well-pressed lieutenant was the representative of interests opposed to those of his nation. Practicality was a supreme virtue in the wilderness, and White Eagle, as the snowy-haired McLoughlin was known to the Indians, had made a small fortune for himself and his company through the sale of supplies to the flood of American settlers that had entered the region over the past few years.

Once the entire party was reunited at the camp above the Dalles where Frémont had left Carson, Fitzpatrick, and the others, Frémont announced that they would not be returning directly via the Oregon Trail, as his orders prescribed, but would instead head south to explore the Great Basin region. The wisdom of heading out for uncharted regions with winter coming was certainly open to question, but Frémont claimed that his men welcomed the challenge. Although exploring the Great Basin was in itself a legitimate scientific objective (albeit one perhaps best left for a different time of year), it appears that Frémont's specific motivation was his desire to find the Buenaventura River, a mythical waterway said to traverse the Great Basin and link the Rockies with the San Francisco Bay.

It was 26 degrees and snowing when the expedition left the Dalles at daybreak on November 25. The weather did not improve as winter drew on, and the party was often able to make only seven or eight miles per day. They passed through a divide in the Cascade Mountains and continued south, the rugged Sierra Nevada to their west, the forbidding waste of the Great Basin to the east. At Klamath Lake, some Klamath Indians provided them with dried fish and warned them not to attempt to cross the mountains in the winter. In some places, the horses damaged their hooves on sharp lava deposits, the remnants of the region's

(continued on page 52)

A 19th-century artist's etching of Mount Hood as seen from the Columbia River. As they tramped doggedly toward Fort Vancouver, Frémont's men enjoyed a similar view.

The Mormon Trail

The Oregon Trail began either at Westport or Independence, Missouri, followed the Platte and North Platte rivers north by northwest to Fort Laramie in present-day Wyoming, crossed the Rockies at South Pass, and veered southward to Fort Bridger before winding northwest again to the Oregon Territory. In the 1840s, thousands of pioneers traveled its length, many of them carrying all their worldly possessions in covered Conestoga wagons, hoping, in the words of Lansford Hastings's *Emigrants' Guide to Oregon and California*, published in 1845, to turn Oregon's "wild forests, trackless plains, untrodden valleys" into "one grand scene of continuous improvements, universal enterprise, and unparalleled commerce."

Not all of those who set off along the Oregon Trail into the western wilderness had Oregon as their ultimate destination. Among the most unusual of the emigrants were the Mormons, as the members of the Church of Jesus Christ of Latter-Day Saints are known. Most of the Mormons were bound not for Oregon's fertile Willamette Valley but for the area surrounding the Great Salt Lake in the northeast reaches of the Great Basin, an arid region shunned by most settlers. Collectively, the Mormon emigrants, in the words of historian James M. McPherson, constituted the "most remarkable westward migration before the California gold rush of 1849."

The Mormon church was founded in upstate New York in 1830 by Joseph Smith, a 24-year-old Vermonter who asserted that an angel, Moroni, had disclosed to him the location of a book of gold plates, written in an ancient language akin to Egyptian, that contained divine revelation. With the aid of two magical stones, Smith was able to decipher its message. *The Book of Mormon*, Smith's translation of this scripture, revealed that Smith had been chosen as the prophet of a new church. Along with the Bible, Smith's translations and writings—the Book of Mormon, *Doctrine and Covenants*, and *The Pearl of Great Price*—are believed by Mormons to be God's direct revelation to the faithful.

The charismatic Smith quickly won a sizable following, including another Vermonter, Brigham Young, but Mormon practices stirred the suspicion and hostility of their neighbors. The first Mormon communities were communally organized, and their economic success aroused envy. Mormons shunned caffeine, alcohol, tobacco, and all stimulants; their constant proselytizing and assertion that theirs was the only true religion enraged Protestants and Catholics, and their insistence on following the law as laid down by Smith, which in some cases conflicted with civil codes, angered government authorities. Most outrageous to outsiders was the Mormon sanction of polygamy. Persecution drove the Mormons ever westward, first to Ohio, then to Missouri, where they engaged in several pitched battles with the state militia, and then to Illinois, where Smith, who had been jailed for his defiance of state authority, was seized and murdered by an irate mob. With the prophet's death, control of the church passed to Brigham Young, who believed that the unsettled West was the best place for the faithful. Attracted by Frémont's glowing reports of the Great Salt Lake region, in 1846–47 Young led his flock west. What became known as the Mormon Trail branched off to the southwest from the Oregon

Trail at Fort Bridger. Most Mormons stopped at the settlement that would become known as Salt Lake City; others continued on to the southwest through the Great Basin, extending the Mormon Trail to southern California. Although Young disagreed with Frémont's assessment of Utah's potential, saying bluntly that the area was a desert and that had he known as much he would have headed elsewhere, the Mormons used sophisticated irrigation techniques to make the wasteland bloom; by 1860, 40,000 of the faithful had followed the Mormon Trail to the Great Basin. Their success, coupled with Frémont's reports, made Utah attractive to other settlers; it became the 45th state in 1896.

Brigham Young led the Mormons west to the Great Salt Lake region after the death of Joseph Smith.

(continued from page 49)

volcanic past. In other areas, the rough terrain gave way to sand covered with a fine salt where nothing grew. All the time the weather grew colder. On Christmas Day, Frémont poured out shots of brandy and fired the howitzer in an attempt to rally his flagging men. There was, of course, no sign of the Buenaventura, but Frémont remained undaunted, displaying the unflappable optimism that some critics denounced as foolhardiness but that won him the loyalty of many who served under him.

Spirits were raised temporarily when the group came upon Pyramid Lake, so called because of a rock formation of that shape that rose 600 feet above the lake's surface. The Paiute Indians they met there were friendly and gladly gave the explorers trout and other food to eat, but they laughed and shook their heads when asked if they would be willing to guide the whites west across the Sierra Nevada and into California. Uncertain as to where to find a pass through the mountains, Frémont continued to head south.

By January 18, as the party made camp near the Carson River, south of Pyramid Lake, it was clear that a new

An interior view of Fort Vancouver, the Hudson's Bay Company's outpost on the Columbia River. Inside its fortified gates were all the stores and services of a medium-sized town, including a blacksmith, two churches, a school, a livery, a granary, and a jail.

course of action had to be determined. The men were hungry and tired, all too aware that no one, least of all Frémont, really knew where they were going. Their horses were gaunt, skeletal even, and many of them were limping with broken hooves and bruised pasterns and fetlocks. Five of the expedition's mules had collapsed and had to be abandoned in the snow. Rejecting the alternative of spending the winter at Pyramid Lake, Frémont opted to set out immediately across the rugged Sierra Nevada, beyond which, he hoped, lay the lush Sacramento Valley. Frémont later wrote that his "decision was heard with joy by the people, and diffused new life throughout the camp."

If such was the case, the optimism soon vanished. Within a week the party was lashed by a tremendous snowstorm, and on January 26 Preuss confided to his diary that "we still do not know where we really are." Snowshoed Washo Indians encountered along the West Walker River indicated that it was impossible to cross over the mountains. The whites pushed on. Several days later an elderly

Preuss' sketch of the Frémont party at Pyramid Lake in western Nevada. Note the Pathfinder's tepee, the howitzer that the expedition had dragged all the way from Westport, and the strange triangular tufa formation, 600 feet high, for which the lake was named.

Washo tried to convince them of their folly. "Rock upon rock—rock upon rock—snow upon snow—snow upon snow," Frémont recorded the Washo as saying, "even if you get over the snow, you will not be able to get down from the mountains." These words caused a Chinook Indian who had traveled with the party since the Oregon Territory to despair. Tearfully, he lamented, "I wanted to see the whites. I came away from my own people to see the whites, and I wouldn't care to die among them."

On February 6, Frémont and Carson discovered a pass through the Sierra Nevada, located somewhere between present-day Markleeville, California, and Lake Tahoe. In a tent in the expedition's base camp, Preuss wrote, "For two days now we have been camping on the slope of a mountain crest. Snow prevents us from moving on. . . . Today the 'field marshal' [one of Preuss' sarcastic nicknames for Frémont] marched out with a party on snowshoes to open a way to the summit, about 10 miles distant, it appears. Tomorrow we shall probably know whether it is possible to get through. The men had to work terribly hard to drag the baggage up the steep mountain; the beasts are too weak for it. Two of them rolled down the snow about 200 feet. No longer any salt in camp. This is awful." Preuss' mood did not improve any when he learned that his favorite mule, Jack, had been slaughtered to take its place in the communal stewpot along with the expedition's mascot, a dog named Tlamath. On the verge of physical collapse, the exhausted and badly undernourished Preuss was unable to assist with the grueling work of breaking a trail through the snowy pass. Instead, he found himself assigned to the kitchen tent and the preparation of Jack and Tlamath. He consoled himself by reading Lord Byron's epic poem *Don Juan* while stirring the broth that contained their remains.

Several more weeks of hardship followed. The difficulty of crossing the mountains even convinced Frémont to abandon his beloved howitzer. A number of men contracted frostbite, and one individual, crazed by hunger and fatigue, simply wandered off from the party into the snowy wastes, but by the end of February the worst was over and the party was descending into the fertile Sacramento Valley. The mountains were less rugged on the California side, and only patches of snow hindered their progress, although a number of pack animals, including the mule that carried Frémont's plant specimens, tumbled off the precarious trail and were lost. On the evening of March 4, they camped on the shore of the Sacramento River where, as Frémont wrote, "the associated beauties of scenery made so strong an impression on us that we have given it the name of the Beautiful Camp." Many species of colorful wildflowers dotted the rolling foothills, and wild game roamed peacefully nearby in large herds. At Sutter's Fort, a trading post established near the confluence of the Sacramento and American rivers five years earlier by John Sutter, a Swiss immigrant who had made a fortune as a trader and rancher, the ragged band was treated to a feast served on European-made china by Indian servants that included trout, salmon, duck, geese, quail, ham, beef, fresh vegetables, fruit, cheese, milk, coffee, and wine.

By March 22, Frémont and his men were sufficiently rejuvenated to begin the long trek home. (Frémont's de-

Frémont's attempt to cross the snowy Sierra Nevada in wintertime was a mistake, but not one that he learned from. His next attempt to make a winter crossing of a western mountain range would be much more costly. This illustration is from Frémont's report to Congress.

termination to depart was reinforced by a dispute he had with Sutter over some stolen sugar and Sutter's bill for the supplies the expedition purchased.) Rather than cross the Sierra Nevada again, the expedition headed south through the San Joaquin Valley, where colorful wildflowers were blossoming and herds of antelope, deer, and wild horses grazed on the slopes. At night the men could hear the howling of wolves and coyotes, and they came upon much evidence of the presence of bears. At the Mojave River they turned east, intending to follow a well-marked route known as the Old Spanish Trail across the Mojave Desert.

The desert proved to be no less harrowing than the Sierra Nevada had been. The men were discouraged by the bleakness of the landscape and the sparseness of game after the rich valley, and their spirits dropped even more when they came across two Mexicans, a boy and a man, who told them that their party had been the victims of some horse-stealing Paiute. Carson and Alexis Godey, one of the expedition's ablest hunters, immediately rode out after the Indians. They returned the next day with two Indian scalps and a graphic tale of the slaughter. Preuss was appalled, both at Carson and Godey's bloodlust and at the apparent indifference of the rest of the group. He recorded in his diary that he believed Frémont would gladly have traded all his scientific specimens from the journey to have been with the two avengers.

Paiute continued to menace the band as it worked its way northeast, along a course west of but roughly parallel to that of the Virgin River. At one point a large band of Paiute warriors—Frémont called them "wolves of the desert"—surrounded the expedition's encampment. A tense night followed, with the Indians proclaiming their contempt for the whites' rifles and strolling brazenly through the explorers' camp while Carson threatened to shoot their chief through the head. The expedition proceeded tensely across the southern end of the Great Basin, with the men gradually becoming aware that they had lost the traces of

(continued on page 65)

Visions of the West

Bass Otis's 1856 portrait of John Frémont hangs in the National Portrait Gallery in Washington, D.C.

In many ways, artists did as much as explorers to open the American West. Many Americans derived their vision of the West's native inhabitants and breathtaking landscapes from the paintings, drawings, and sketches of such accomplished artists as George Catlin, George Caleb Bingham, Karl Bodmer, Alfred Jacob Miller, Emanuel Leutze, Charles M. Russell, Albert Bierstadt, and others. Particularly in the years before photographs were widely circulated, the work of these men constituted the most complete visual record of the West. That in many cases this work was romanticized and politicized did not lessen its appeal; Americans wanted to feel good about westward expansion, and the notion that the West was a place of singular beauty and exoticism accorded well with the optimism of a confident young nation convinced that it was special. In a period that is inundated with photographic, cinematic, and televised images, Bingham's and Miller's fur traders, Catlin's and Bodmer's Indians, Russell's cowboys, and Bierstadt's mountains remain archetypes of the unsettled American West.

Emanuel Leutze's Across the Continent, Westward the Course of Empire Takes Its Way *is a mural measuring 20 by 30 feet that hangs in the U.S. Capitol. The German-born Leutze was completely taken by America's democratic energy; he was equally famous for his other great work,* Washington Crossing the Delaware. *In this heroic evocation of America fulfilling its Manifest Destiny, Leutze intended, in his own words, "to represent as nearly and truthfully as the artist was able the grand peaceful conquest of the Great West." Note the Frémont figure in the background atop the peak.*

This contemporary map of the Oregon Trail captures much of the scope and sweep of the United States's great western adventure.

Charles Preuss drew this map of Oregon and California after returning from Frémont's second expedition.

Albert Bierstadt's The Rocky Mountains—Lander's Peak *was
the prime attraction at the New York Sanitary Fair Exhibition
of 1864, which was held to raise funds for medical treatment of
the Civil War wounded. Historian William H. Goetzmann
wrote that with this painting Bierstadt "became the orchestrator
of a mighty, Wagnerian scene, which exaggerated the vertical
thrust of the Wind River Range to achieve the monumental
grandeur which Americans had come to expect from their
continent."*

The Green River in Utah, by Rudolf Cronau. The work of the western artists gave form to the topographic details hinted at by cartographers and fleshed out the words of the West's prose chroniclers.

Carson and His Men, *by Charles M. Russell. A descendant of the Bents, fur traders and proprietors of Bent's Fort, Russell ran away from his St. Louis family in 1880 at the age of 16. He spent the next several years working as a cowboy and hunter before achieving success as an artist. Russell is best known for his portrayals of cowboys and his sympathetic treatment of the Indians, whom he called the "true Americans."*

*The United States as it existed in 1850.
Thirteen states would come from the
regions explored by Frémont.*

(continued from page 56)

the Old Spanish Trail. As neither Carson nor Fitzpatrick had been in this country before, there was just cause for apprehension.

At an encampment near present-day Newcastle, Utah, in the southeastern portion of the state, Frémont's men were surprised by the arrival of nine men on horseback. Carson and Fitzpatrick were overjoyed, for this party's leader was none other than Joseph Walker, the veritable exemplar of the mountain man. Frémont was already engaged in building the legend that would lead an adoring public to call him the Pathfinder, but if anyone had earned that sobriquet, it was Walker. One year older than the century, Walker had covered more of the West than any man alive. In 1833 he had led a party of 40 individuals from the Green River country across the Great Basin and the Sierra Nevada through California to the sparkling waters of the San Francisco Bay. En route, Walker's party had become the first white men to visit the magnificent Yosemite Valley. In the years since, Walker had added to his reputation. It was said of him that he "didn't follow trails, but rather made them," and stories of Walker appearing seemingly out of nowhere to rescue travelers from Indians or from their own folly constituted a separate chapter in the lore of the West. The blue-eyed and bearded Walker still cut an impressive figure; his 6-foot frame carried 200 pounds of finely honed muscle, and he wore his straight black hair long, well over his shoulders. Frémont's men greeted him with much joy.

With Walker's help, the party had little difficulty finding their way across the Wasatch and Rocky mountains. On July 1, it reached Bent's Fort. After a festive Fourth of July feast, it was on to Westport, which was reached at the end of July. On August 6, 1844, Frémont disembarked from a steamboat at St. Louis, where Jessie, who had quite literally been worried sick during the 14 months that he had been gone, was waiting at her family's estate.

Alfred Jacob Miller's portrait of Joseph Walker, the mountain man par excellence. Daniel Conner, who accompanied Walker on one of his last expeditions, described him as "the kindest man I ever knew, considering the desperate chances which he had been constantly taking for 30 years amongst the savages, burning deserts, and bleak snows. Brave, truthful, he was as kindly as a child, yet occasionally he was even austere."

CALIFORNIA REPUBLIC

The Bear Flag Rebellion

Frémont spent the next several months getting reacquainted with his family, composing his official report for submission to Congress, and basking in his celebrity, for he was now America's foremost hero. He had much to be proud of, for the recently concluded journey constituted the most comprehensive reconnaissance to date of the entire West. With Jessie again providing invaluable assistance as amanuensis and editor, the completed report, more than 600 pages in length, was presented to Congress on March 1, 1845. As had his previous work, the report combined Frémont's breathless narrative with solid scientific information, maps, sketches, and practical advice for settlers, such as where the best farmland was to be found, the best forts for resupplying along the way, and how to hire a mountain man. The following year, Preuss completed his grandly detailed seven-part map of the Oregon Trail from Westport to Walla Walla; it became, with Frémont's report, the standard guide for pioneers along that route. Although in his report Frémont generally showed great restraint in not discussing areas he had not personally observed, he did make several glaring errors, such as asserting that the freshwater Utah Lake and the Great Salt Lake constituted one body of water.

Nevertheless, the report was a tremendous success. No less an authority than the great Prussian scientist Baron Alexander von Humboldt praised Frémont for his "talent,

This homespun flag, made of unbleached cotton cloth and a piece of red linen from a woman's petticoat, was raised by the American rebels over the Mexican garrison at Sonoma, California, on June 14, 1846.

courage, industry, and enterprise." The Senate ordered 10,000 copies, combined with his first report, printed for sale as A *Report of the Exploring Expedition to the Rocky Mountains in the Year 1842, and to Oregon and North California in the Years 1843–44.* All of them were quickly purchased by an adoring public; several publishing houses, in the United States and Europe, brought out their own versions. In later years critics and even some of Frémont's companions of the trail would charge that he artfully embellished his accounts to create himself a hero, but there is no doubt that Frémont's vision of the West captured the imagination of countless Americans. The poet Joaquin Miller revealed in his autobiography that Frémont's report had a significant impact on his development as a boy growing up in Ohio: "I fancied I could see Frémont's men, hauling the cannon up the savage battlements of the Rocky Mountains, flags in the air, Frémont at the head, waving his sword, his horse neighing wildly in the mountain wind, with unknown and unnamed empires on every hand. . . . I began to be inflamed with a love for action, adventure, glory, and great deeds away out yonder under the path of the setting sun." Frémont's beautiful helpmate reinforced his image as a dashing American hero; together the handsome Frémonts were the optimistic young republic's first

The first section of Preuss' famous seven-section "Topographical Map of the Road from Missouri to Oregon; Commencing at the Mouth of the Kansas in the Missouri River and Ending at the Mouth of the Wallah Wallah in the Columbia."

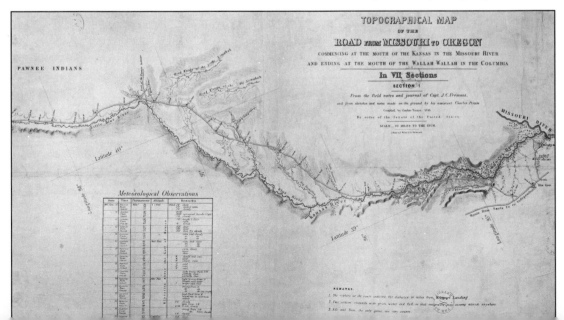

couple. Even the army rewarded its newest star; although Frémont had not attended West Point, he was given a brevet appointment as a captain.

Not all was happiness. Frémont's mentor, Joseph Nicollet, had died while he was away, not, as Frémont believed would have been appropriate, "under the open sky, [where he could] be buried, rolled up in a blanket, by the side of some stream in the mountains," but alone in a hotel room in Washington, D.C. But if Nicollet's end haunted Frémont, it was not readily apparent, for by the spring of 1845 he was busy making plans for his next expedition.

The official orders given Frémont by Colonel Abert were less than ambitious in scope. On this journey, Frémont was to confine himself to surveying the lands along the Arkansas and Red rivers. (The latter constitutes the present border between Oklahoma and Texas.) In his *Memoirs of My Life*, Frémont asserted that he was given the authority to proceed on his own discretion beyond the Rockies and the Sierra Nevada as far west as he deemed prudent. No official document authorizing such a journey has ever been uncovered, and the matter remains open to dispute.

What is obvious is that from the outset Frémont had in mind something far grander than what Abert's written orders authorized him to do. The expedition he put together during a clamorous several weeks in St. Louis in May and June of 1845—his fame was now so great that each time he ventured out in public he was mobbed by men seeking a place on his new expedition—was his largest and best armed. Applicants competed for positions by displaying their marksmanship with a variety of weapons. Several standbys from the first two expeditions, such as Lajeunesse, Godey, and Lucien Maxwell, signed on, and Carson and Walker awaited ahead on the trail. (The strenuous objections of Preuss' wife convinced him to sit this one out; his place was taken by Ned Kern, a long-limbed

Poet Joaquin Miller was one of many thousands of Americans whose imaginations were inflamed by Frémont's heroic accounts of his western adventures.

(continued on page 72)

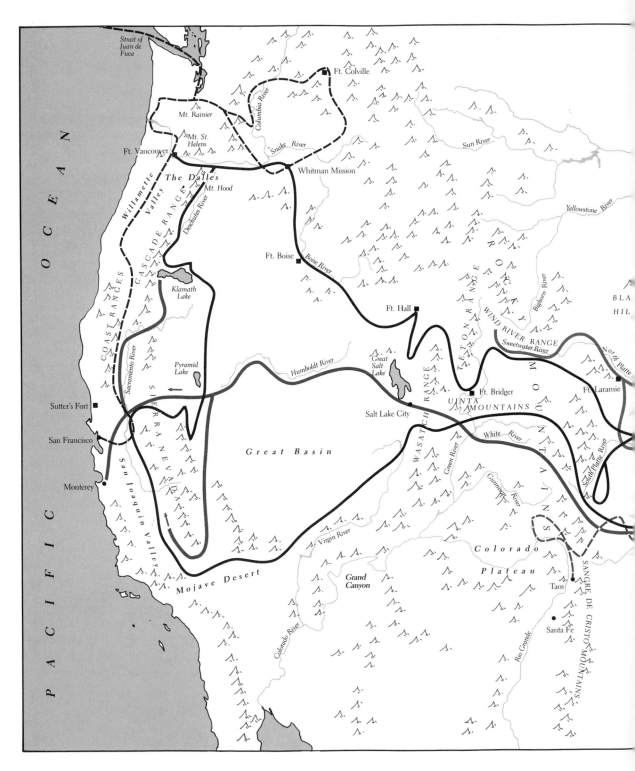

Strait of Juan de Fuca

Ft. Colville

O C E A N

Mt. Rainier

Columbia River

Mt. St. Helens

Snake River

Ft. Vancouver

Whitman Mission

Sun River

Willamette Valley

The Dalles

Mt. Hood

Deschutes River

Yellowstone River

CASCADE RANGE

Ft. Boise

Boise River

Ft. Hall

Klamath Lake

COAST RANGES

Sacramento River

Pyramid Lake

Humboldt River

Great Salt Lake

SIERRA NEVADA

Sutter's Fort

San Francisco

Great Basin

Salt Lake City

Ft. Bridger

UINTA MOUNTAINS

Ft. Laramie

WIND RIVER RANGE

TETON RANGE

ROCKY MOUNTAINS

Bighorn River

North Platte

Sweetwater River

BLA HIL

WASATCH RANGE

White River

Green River

South Platte River

Monterey

San Joaquin Valley

Virgin River

Gunnison River

Colorado Plateau

Mojave Desert

Grand Canyon

Colorado River

Taos

Santa Fe

Rio Grande

SANGRE DE CRISTO MOUNTAINS

P A C I F I C

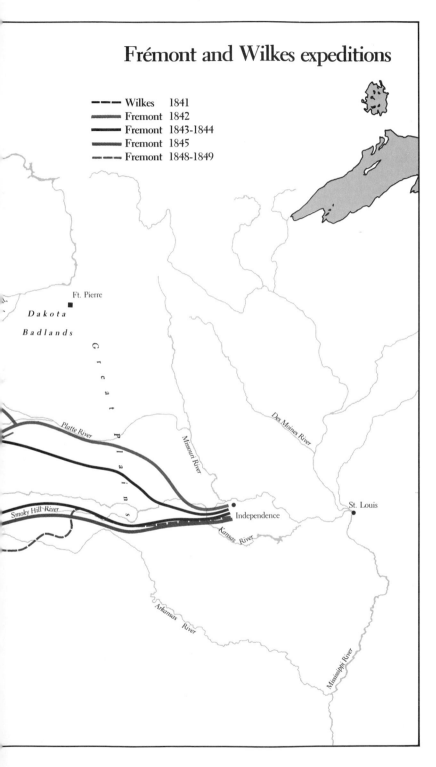

Frémont and Wilkes expeditions

- - - - Wilkes 1841
——— Fremont 1842
——— Fremont 1843-1844
——— Fremont 1845
- - - - Fremont 1848-1849

Ft. Pierre

Dakota

Badlands

G r e a t

P l a i n s

Platte River

Missouri River

Des Moines River

Smoky Hill River

Kansas River

Independence

St. Louis

Arkansas River

Mississippi River

The routes taken by Wilkes while in the West and by Frémont on his first four expeditions.

(continued from page 69)

21-year-old artist.) Those who obtained a coveted spot with Frémont were given to understand that his objective was to cross the Rockies and then the Great Basin, along the route of the Mary's River (renamed the Humboldt by Frémont), and then traverse the Sierra Nevada and enter California's Sacramento Valley.

Surrounded by his personal bodyguard of Delaware Indians, Frémont led his 62-man expedition from its gathering place at Boon's Creek in eastern Kansas in mid-June. They made quick time to Bent's Fort, where they were joined by Fitzpatrick and Carson. Deciding to acknowledge the survey's ostensible purpose, Frémont ordered 34 of his men, under the leadership of Colonel Abert's son, James, to head south and carry out the survey of the Arkansas and Red rivers territory. Once finished, they were to proceed back to St. Louis. Fitzpatrick was deputed to act as their guide.

The remainder of the expedition continued west. At Pueblo they hired on Bill Williams as another guide. Then 59 years old, Old Bill was one of the most eccentric of the fur trappers, known for his love of solitude, his filthiness, his religious mysticism, and his practice of wearing war paint, like an Indian. Mountain men and Indians alike usually gave him a wide berth, for it was said that during his long winters in the mountains he practiced cannibalism. Still, he had the undeniable virtue of having spent years in the wilderness, and Frémont believed he would be helpful in getting them across the Rockies.

Williams did prove useful for that purpose, although he left the group when Frémont announced his intention to cross the barren salt flats west of the Great Salt Lake, a course of action the local Indians advised against as well. His absence was more than made up for by the arrival of the always timely Joseph Walker, and with Carson breaking trail, the party succeeded in traversing the thirsty flats, in the process providing a shorter, alternate route to the California Trail most often used by settlers.

A close friend of Carson's, Lucien B. Maxwell was an extremely skilled hunter and horseman and a valued member of the first three Frémont expeditions.

Wishing to explore as much of the Great Basin as possible, Frémont divided his party in two. The larger group, led by Walker, followed the Humboldt River, while Frémont led his band southwest. By late November, both parties had reached the large lake, in what is now western Nevada, that Frémont named after Walker. His journey across the northern reaches of the Great Basin enabled Frémont to dispel the notion that it was nothing but a "barren and sandy wasteland." The Pathfinder discovered that even the popular notion that it was flat was inaccurate; he was to write later: "Instead of a plain, I found it throughout its whole extent, traversed by parallel ranges of lofty mountains, their summits white with snow. . . . Instead of a barren country, the mountains were covered with grasses of the best quality, wooded with several varieties of trees, and containing more deer and mountain sheep than we had seen in any previous part of our voyage."

At Walker Lake, Frémont again split his party. Walker's group was ordered south, to the lower end of the Sierra Nevada, where they crossed the mountains through what is known today as Walker Pass. Meanwhile, Frémont headed northwest, where he followed the Truckee River

Horsemen enter a valley in the Great Basin. Frémont was the first to make a detailed, scientific exploration of the area; his work demonstrated that the region's topography was much more diverse than was previously believed.

Clouds over Walker Lake, one of the many places in the West named after Joseph Walker, who probably covered more of its terrain than any man.

through the mountains in early December, just beating the winter snows. (A group of settlers that attempted to reach California by this route—known afterward as the Donner Pass—the following winter was not as fortunate. The 87-member Donner party was trapped in the mountains by a series of fierce blizzards. Before their rescue the following spring more than half had perished, and the survivors had resorted to cannibalism to survive.) After a stopover at Sutter's Fort and some skirmishes with horse-stealing Indians, Frémont's party marched south and was reunited with Walker's group in the San Joaquin Valley in February.

California at the time was in tumult, a state of affairs Frémont had no doubt counted on when making it his destination. While still proceeding cautiously, expansionists in the U.S. government, President James Polk among them, had become increasingly open about their desire to wrest California (and other southwestern territory) from Mexico, which, because of an apparent lack of interest, maintained only a tenuous control over it. Mexico's hold was so weak that it was forced to tolerate the presence of a Russian trading post at Fort Ross, on the San Francisco Bay, and U.S., British, and French ships called regularly at California ports, despite the government's official policy of barring foreign vessels. Mexico's power in the region was further sapped by a fierce dispute between its two most important officials there, Juan Alvarado, who headed the civil government from the official capital at Ciudad de los Angeles (City of the Angels, known today as Los Angeles), and José Castro, whose headquarters was at the military garrison at Sonoma and who conducted himself as a sort of military governor. Although Castro did all in his power to discourage American settlement of California, including encouraging the Indians to raid American settlements and restricting American trade privileges, the Americans continued to come, drawn by California's verdant valleys, and by the time of Frémont's arrival the American population there was roughly equal to that of the Mexicans. With rumors flying that armed conflict between Mexico and the United States over the southwest was imminent (indeed, the two nations would go to war in May 1846), Castro quite naturally viewed the arrival of a heavily armed party of rough-and-ready frontiersmen, under the command of a U.S. Army captain, as a provocation.

The central plaza and barracks at Sonoma, the California town where the Osos struck the first blow of the Bear Flag Rebellion.

Western artist Frederic Remington's painting of government scouts breaking trail. Carson and Frémont's other guides probably dressed similarly to these men.

Frémont, on his part, wasted little time in acting provocatively. When a Mexican government official protested over Frémont's insulting treatment of a Mexican citizen who alleged that one of Frémont's men had stolen his horse, Frémont responded with a caustic letter to the official in which he charged that the accuser "should have been well satisfied to escape without a severe horse-whipping." He imperiously added that he regretted that he would not be able to meet with the official to discuss the matter but trusted that his correspondent would "readily understand that my duties will not permit me to appear before the magistrates of your towns on the complaint of every straggling vagabond who may chance to visit my camp."

Such high-handedness, as well as Frémont's secretive meetings with the American consul, Thomas Larkin, at Monterey, did not sit well with Castro, who suspected, perhaps accurately, that Frémont had been dispatched by the U.S. government to foment unrest among the Americans and even possibly to act as an invasion force in case of war. (Frémont always maintained that he had been authorized by the government to go to California, although no documents to that effect have ever been unearthed. It is certain that no one attempted to recall him once it was learned that he was there.) Castro summarily ordered Frémont and his men from the colony.

Frémont refused to comply. Instead, he ordered his men to build a log fort on Hawk's Peak, north of Monterey, where in early March 1846 they provocatively raised the Stars and Stripes. American settlers eager to see California free of Mexico journeyed to the redoubt to volunteer their services, while in the valley below Castro prepared his forces for an assault. During the tense standoff that followed, both sides tried to outdo the other in bellicose rhetoric. Perhaps realizing that his current stand far exceeded whatever authorization, if any, he had been

granted, Frémont withdrew his forces on March 9 and headed north to Oregon.

Frémont's capitulation cost him the services of Walker, who had long been fascinated by California and believed the Americans should take it. In later years he was even more scathing than Preuss in his assessment of the Path-finder: "Frémont morally and physically was the most complete coward I ever knew, and if it were not casting an unmerited reproach on the sex I would say that he was more timid than a woman. An explorer! I knew more of the unexplored region 15 years before he set foot on it than he does today."

Whether other members of Frémont's party were also disappointed is unknown, but events seem to indicate that by the time the group reached the upper Sacramento Valley they were spoiling for a fight. When some newly arrived settlers asked the armed band for protection against some allegedly hostile Indians, probably Klamath, a massacre ensued. Led by Carson, the initial rifle assault on a nearby Indian village killed 24 tribesmen; 3 hours of hand-to-hand combat resulted in the death of more than 150 other

Preuss' drawing of a friendly meeting with Indians at Upper Klamath Lake. Later encounters were more bellicose.

This rendering of an Indian ambush illustrated the memoirs of one of the survivors of the ill-starred Donner party. The ambush of Basil Lajeunesse by a Klamath brave put the already bloodthirsty men of Frémont's third expedition into a murderous frenzy.

Native Americans. Frémont's band apparently escaped unscathed. The explorers celebrated this "perfect butchery" (Carson's words) with two days of drinking and dancing at an emigrant encampment in the vicinity.

On the night of May 8, while the band was encamped near Klamath Lake, they were visited by two hard-riding horsemen, who told Frémont that they had been sent ahead by a Lieutenant Archibald Gillespie, who had important orders for him. Fully aware that the Indians in the territory through which Gillespie would have to pass were likely to be less than hospitable, the next day Frémont led a rescue party south. After a long day's ride, they found Gillespie and three others, unharmed, in the vicinity of the Klamath River. There, Gillespie passed on to Frémont orders from Polk, Secretary of State James Buchanan, Secretary of the Navy George Bancroft, and Senator Benton. The exact nature of the communication is unknown, but Frémont did begin planning immediately to march back

to California. Excited, perhaps overtired from the strenuous ride, he forgot to post sentries around the camp. In
the darkness after midnight, a Klamath warrior slew the
sleeping Lajeunesse with a tomahawk. Although the
whites and their Delaware allies were able to fight off the
raiding party, it cost them two men. A Klamath chieftain
was also killed. Carson later pronounced him the bravest
warrior he had seen, but in the immediate aftermath of
the skirmish he found no cause for praise. Incensed at his
comrades' death, Carson smashed the Klamath's skull to
bits with an ax.

Revenge did not stop there. Before heading south for
California, the reunited party laid siege to a Klamath village at Upper Klamath Lake. That it was uncertain that
their attackers had hailed from this settlement did not
lessen the ferocity of the Frémont party's assault. After
driving the Klamath from their homes, in the process
killing more than a score, the whites put the village to the
torch.

The killing did not cease with Frémont's return to California. Suspecting that as the tension between the Americans and the Mexicans escalated, Castro would encourage
the Indians to harass American settlers, Frémont determined to terrorize the Indian population into quiescence.
As he put it years later in his *Memoirs*: "I resolved to
anticipate the Indians and strike them a blow which would
make them recognize that Castro was far and that I was
near." To that end, Frémont and his men laid waste all
the villages of the Maidu Indians—a placid people the
whites contemptuously called Diggers because of their
practice of digging for roots and other foodstuffs—along
the Sacramento River between the Mokelumne and Cal-
averas rivers, slaughtering their inhabitants and burning
their dwellings.

Emboldened by Frémont's arrival, a motley assemblage
of hunters, trappers, and settlers, led by a colorful gray-
haired mountain man known as "Stuttering" Ezekiel Mer-

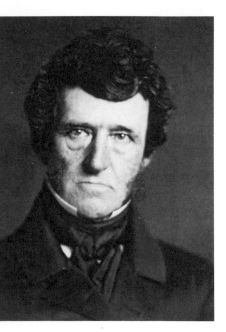

Commodore Robert Stockton took command of the U.S. forces in California in the summer of 1846; he pronounced California U.S. territory on August 17. Frémont enjoyed an easy rapport with the charismatic, impulsive Stockton.

ritt, prepared to take action against the Mexicans. In mid-June 1846, with the tacit approval of Frémont, the Osos, as they called themselves, overran the Mexican garrison at Sonoma, announced that California would from that point on be an independent republic, and hoisted a crude white flag, made from a piece of cotton and embellished with a single red star, the figure of a bear, and the words CALIFORNIA REPUBLIC in black. (Oso is the Spanish word for bear; the rebels settled on it as their name because both the Mexicans and the Americans respected the fighting prowess of the grizzly.) The Osos were heartened by the almost immediate arrival of American warships, commanded by Commodore Robert Stockton, at Monterey, and the news that a U.S. Army division, commanded by Frémont's old nemesis in the affair of the howitzer, Stephen Kearny, now a brigadier general, was on the march to San Diego. Encouraged himself, Frémont now proposed to the Osos that he merge his group with them and become their commanding officer. The Osos agreed, and Stockton subsequently confirmed Frémont as the commander of the California Battalion, as the new force was known, in the process promoting him to major.

The only problem with Stockton's action was that his authority was open to question. A navy officer had no power to promote an army man, or give orders to him, and when Kearny, a by-the-rules stickler, arrived, he let Stockton, and Frémont, know it. In the meantime, after several months of skirmishes, the Mexicans surrendered. California was in need of a temporary government until such time as steps could be taken to join it to the United States, and as he had hinted he would do, Stockton appointed Frémont governor, in January 1847. Kearny protested, loudly and clearly, that he had orders from the president that gave him the sole authority in California. He also gave Frémont a direct order that he was not to relinquish command of the California Battalion and assume the governorship. Sure of himself as ever, perhaps even more so in the wake of all his recent triumphs, the Pathfinder defied his superior officer and did just the opposite.

For a little more than a month, Frémont acted on his own authority as governor of California. The new government needed money, so Frémont personally took on the more than $600,000 in debt it incurred, including a not insubstantial sum for the purchase of the island of Alcatraz. Kearny continued to fulminate, until in late March Frémont learned that Kearny had been officially appointed governor by General Winfield Scott, the head of the army. Frémont was ordered to muster the California Battalion into the United States Army, a directive he defied. He then compounded his indiscretion by challenging Colonel Richard Mason, who had been sent by Washington to relieve Kearny, to a duel. In late May, Kearny presented Frémont with orders he did not dare refuse. Frémont and all the members of his topographic expedition, except those who wished to stay in California, were to return to Washington with Kearny. His specimens and scientific equipment were to be turned over to army officers in California.

A somewhat chastened Frémont set out with Kearny and his soldiers in early June 1847. Most of the trip was uneventful, except for the passage through the Donner Pass, where in rude cabins the travelers discovered grisly evidence of the tragedy that had befallen the unfortunate emigrants the previous winter—skulls, other bones, and bits of flesh. (Later, both Kearny and Frémont charged that the other refused to help with the task of giving these remains a burial.) Although Frémont was aware that upon his arrival home this time he was likely to receive a somewhat different reception in the halls of government than he had before, he was nonetheless shocked when at Fort Leavenworth, on the west bank of the Missouri River in present-day Kansas, Kearny announced that he should consider himself under arrest for the crime of mutiny.

Brigadier General Stephen Watts Kearny, Frémont's nemesis, despised the Pathfinder, whose flamboyant ways he regarded as the antithesis of the discipline expected of the responsible army officer. Like many other army officers who had graduated from West Point, Kearny resented the spectacular success enjoyed by Frémont, who had not attended the U.S. Military Academy.

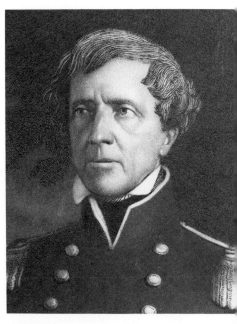

The Winter Disaster

The arrest of Lieutenant Colonel John Charles Frémont (he had been promoted again before the dispute with Kearny), the Pathfinder, the trailblazer of Manifest Destiny, the man whose name, according to one wildly enthusiastic journalist, would be "immortalized among the great travelers and explorers, and will doubtless survive as long as those of the Sierra Nevada and the Sacramento," was front-page news across America. Crowds of supporters lined the banks of the Missouri River between Westport and St. Louis and chanted his name and waved American flags as the steamboat carrying him to justice passed by. In St. Louis, high society rallied behind the Frémonts, and they were invited to numerous dinners and soirees in their honor. (Most of the invitations were declined on the grounds that Frémont needed to devote his time to preparing for trial.) Strangers stopped the Pathfinder on the street to express their assurance that the scandalous charges would be dismissed.

The court-martial took place in Washington, D.C., from November 2, 1847, until the last day of January 1848. Frémont was specifically charged with three offenses, ranging in seriousness from mutiny to disobedience of the lawful command of his superior officer to conduct to the prejudice of good order and military discipline. The judge advocate granted Frémont's request that reporters be admitted to the trial, but he cautioned them that they were not to publish testimony, a stipulation whose letter the

Many Americans regarded it as inconceivable that the heroic Lieutenant Colonel John Charles Frémont could be tried for mutiny.

press found easy to adhere to while violating its spirit for the edification of curious readers. Journalists filled to overflowing the 200-seat gallery set aside for spectators in the Washington Armory, the building where the court-martial was held.

Frémont's defense centered on proving that Kearny had plotted to place him in a situation where he was trapped between the conflicting demands of his rightful superior officer and Stockton. Acting as his own attorney, he also sought to demonstrate that because on many issues Kearny had deferred to Stockton from the time of the general's arrival in California, treating the commodore as if he in fact wielded the supreme authority there, he, Frémont, had quite naturally done the same. Most observers agreed that Frémont achieved his aims. His cross-examination was also successful in demonstrating that Kearny possessed a faulty, if not willfully selective, memory, but the 12 officers who constituted Frémont's jury were not able to overlook Frémont's defiance and delivered a curious verdict. They pronounced him guilty on all three counts and sentenced him to dismissal from the army, but in recognition of the considerable services he had rendered to his country, six of the jurors recommended that President Polk review the sentence. In their statement to the president, the jurors all but acknowledged Frémont's version of events and advised leniency:

> Under the circumstances in which Lieutenant Colonel Frémont was placed between two officers of superior rank, each claiming to command-in-chief in California— circumstances in their nature calculated to embarrass the mind and excite the doubts of officers of greater experience than the accused—and in consideration of the important professional services rendered by him previous to the occurrence of those acts for which he has been tried, the undersigned members of the court, respectfully commend Lieutenant Colonel Frémont to the lenient consideration of the President of the United States.

Polk's judgment was equally indecisive. The president avowed that he considered the evidence to be insufficient to convict Frémont of mutiny but that it supported the lesser two charges. Accordingly, he upheld the verdict of the court on those particulars, but he believed its sentence to be too harsh, and he restored Frémont's commission.

Benton regarded the president's decision as at least a partial vindication of his son-in-law, but Frémont was indignant. From the time of Kearny's stunning announcement, he had regarded his arrest and trial as a supreme insult, and his ego and pride would not let him accept anything less than a total exoneration. Permanently embittered, he resigned his commission. The conviction and loss of his career were a stunning blow, but Frémont managed to look forward. He was not just an army officer, but an explorer, and Benton was already hinting that businessmen interested in investing in a St. Louis to the Pacific railroad wished to hire him to survey a route. The report of his latest expedition also had to be written. Although not as comprehensive as his earlier efforts, *Geographical Memoir upon Upper California, in Illustration of His Map of Oregon and California* was still well received by Congress, which ordered 20,000 copies published for sale to the public. There was also Jessie, whose health had been weakened by the stress of the recent crisis, to look after, as well as his new son, Benton, who was born on July 24, 1848.

But the pleasures of hearth and kin could not long hold the still footloose Frémont, and when Benton told him that the St. Louis investors had agreed to fund his expedition, he made plans to head west. This journey would represent a new beginning for the Frémont family, for near the end of his stay in California in 1847, Frémont had authorized the American consul there, Thomas Larkin, to purchase for him a 40,000-acre ranch located near the Yosemite Valley. He hoped to make Las Mariposas, as the sprawling estate was known, the new family home,

(continued on page 88)

The drawings of Edward "Ned" Kern illustrated Frémont's report of his third expedition.

Historian in the Wild

The great American historian Francis Parkman, Jr., traveled the Oregon Trail in 1846. The bookish 22-year-old New Englander, the descendant of Unitarian ministers and prosperous merchants, did not intend to resettle in the West but rather to fulfill the dream of exploring the wilderness that had obsessed him since his youth. He hoped as well to gather material for the historical work that would make his reputation: an epic history of the struggle between the French and English for control of colonial North America. High-strung and frail, at times nearly blind, plagued by excruciating headaches, Parkman also wished to exorcise the specter of infirmity by testing himself physically, so as to prove the truth of his belief that the "hero is greater than the poet." Among the supplies this unlikely explorer carried with him on the trail were three weighty volumes—the Bible and the collected works of Shakespeare and Lord Byron.

Parkman's account of his journey was published as *The California and Oregon Trail* in 1849. A precise if caustic observer and an elegant, romantic literary stylist, Parkman created some of the most enduring prose images of the way west. Among the subjects that interested him most were the Indians. Like most whites of the day, Parkman saw them as uncivilized savages, although not without their virtues; but he also realized that their way of life had been made meaner by its ongoing destruction. Parkman's Indians were not romanticized. For each Sioux warrior that appears in the pages of his narrative resembling an "Apollo of bronze" and speaking with "a voice like an organ," there is an emaciated squaw, an "old hag of 80. You could count all her ribs through the wrinkles of her leathery skin." The squaw's voice, Parkman notes, resembles the scream of a screech owl. He predicts the ultimate extinction of the buffalo and with it the end of the Indian "communities who depend on them for support. . . . The Indians will soon be abased by whiskey and overawed by military posts." Yet Parkman's harsh vision is tempered somewhat by his realization that "civilization" contains its own discontents:

Never have I seen in any Indian village on the remote prairies such depravity, such utter abasement and prostitution of every nobler part of humanity, as I have seen in great cities, the centres of the world's wisdom and refinement.

Parkman saved his idealizing for the voyageur who guided him west, Henry Chatillon. His initial description of Chatillon remains a powerful evocation of the romantic view of the West of which Frémont was both symbol and creator:

His age was about 30; he was 6 feet high, and very powerfully and gracefully moulded. The prairies had been his school; he could neither read nor write, but he had a natural refinement and delicacy of mind. . . . He was content to take things as he found them; and his chief fault arose from an excess of easy generosity, impelling him to give away too profusely ever to thrive in the world. Yet it was commonly remarked of him, that whatever he might choose to do with what belonged to himself, the property of others was always safe in his hands. . . . It is characteristic of him that in a country where the rifle is the chief arbiter between man and man, Henry was very seldom involved in quarrels. Once or twice, indeed, his quiet good nature had been mistaken and presumed upon, but the consequences of the error were so formidable that no one was ever known to repeat it. No better evidence of the intrepidity of his temper could be wished, than the common report that he had killed more than 30 grizzly bears. He was a proof of what unaided nature will sometimes do.

The American historian Francis Parkman, Jr. The great novelist Herman Melville complimented Parkman's account of the Oregon Trail as having "true wild-game flavor."

(continued from page 85)

a place where he and Jessie could forget about the humiliation he had endured back east. News that gold had been discovered on his acreage only increased his and Jessie's desire to relocate.

In the autumn of 1848 Frémont prepared to make his departure. His underwriters were more frugal than the U.S. government had been, so he was only able to hire on 22 men, but as several were veterans of previous trips—Preuss, Kern, and Godey among them—he considered the expedition well manned. Jessie intended to make the long steamboat journey to Panama, then cross the isthmus and board another ship for the voyage to California, but first she was determined to see off her husband at Westport. Unfortunately, young Benton, who had been born frail, expired on the journey. In this atmosphere of sorrow and ill omens, Frémont bid farewell to Jessie on October 20 and rode off one more time to the West.

Perhaps Frémont had begun to believe the Pathfinder legend that he had so skillfully helped to create, or perhaps the strain of his recent setbacks had left him unable to focus as fully as he should have on details, or perhaps he

Even in temperate weather, the rugged San Juan Mountains presented a severe challenge to overland travelers; few were foolhardy enough to attempt them in wintertime.

believed that he needed to perform the most spectacular feat of his career in order to vindicate himself; for whatever reason, the expedition was extremely ill conceived. So as to prove incontrovertibly that the Rockies need not stand as an insurmountable obstacle to any transcontinental railroad venture, Frémont proposed to cross the range in the dead of winter. The lessons of the winter crossing of the Sierra Nevada on the second expedition were apparently forgotten. And no Carson or Walker, with their intuitive and mysterious sense of direction, waited ahead on the trail; Frémont set out without securing his party the services of an experienced guide.

By the time they reached Bent's Fort on November 15, the weather had turned frigid and there was already three feet of snow on the ground. Frémont wrote to his father-in-law about the conditions but remained undaunted:

> Both Indians and whites here report the snow to be deeper in the mountains than has for a long time been known so early in the season and they predict a severe winter. This morning, for the first time, the mountains showed themselves covered with snow, as well as the country around us; for it has snowed the greater part of yesterday and the night before. They look imposing and somewhat stern; still I am in nowise discouraged, and believe we shall succeed in forcing our way across.

However, at the conclusion of his letter, he did confide to Benton that this might be his last expedition. "It needs strong incitements to undergo the hardships and denial of this kind of life," he wrote, "and as I find I have these no longer, I will drop into a quiet life."

Frémont planned on a route that would take his band between the Arkansas River and the Rio Grande, along roughly the 37th parallel, which today forms the boundary between Colorado and New Mexico. This would require him to cross the San Juan Mountains, in present-day southwest Colorado, and the Wasatch range, in south-central Utah, before reaching the Great Basin. The mule

Frémont expedition veterans Jerome Davis (left) and Thomas Breckenridge posed for this photograph years after their trailbreaking days were over. Breckenridge was among the survivors of the catastrophic fourth expedition; in 1896 he published an account of it.

Frémont's men had not been long in the San Juan Mountains before they realized the folly of their leader's plan. Pack animals collapsed and died in the freezing canyons, and the expedition's members were forced to use their beasts of burden for food.

skinners and mountain men he spoke to at Bent's Fort sought to convince him that his plan was folly, but Frémont would not be dissuaded, declaring that he would be in California in 35 days. As none of these intrepid outdoorsmen could be persuaded to sign on as guide, Frémont was forced to move on to Pueblo in search of a pilot.

There he found his man, in the person of "Old Bill" Williams, whose abrupt departure at the edge of the Great Salt Desert on the previous expedition showed either a want of resolution in the face of adversity or a most thoughtful prudence. In either case, the willingness of this veteran wilderness campaigner to sign on with Frémont's expedition seemed reinforcement of the Pathfinder's belief that his scheme was possible. At a tiny settlement called Hardscrabble, 25 miles up the Arkansas from Pueblo, Frémont gave his men an inspirational speech, bucking them up for the assault on the wintry peaks.

Less than three weeks later, in mid-December, these same men were in fear for their lives. Eleven thousand feet above sea level in the San Juan Mountains, the temperature was 20 degrees below zero. Snow fell almost every day; 10 feet of it lay on the ground, and 10 times that much was piled up in drifts in the canyons. The expedition's mules had begun to sicken and die, which at least saved the men the trouble of killing them, for their flesh was all that stood between the explorers and starvation. Preuss' journal entry for December 17 captured the grim situation: "Hands, and feet, ears and noses, of some people were frozen. That old fool Bill [Williams] lay down and wanted to die just at the summit. Many animals perished here." Most of the men were by this point suffering from frostbite; many also had snow blindness. Altitude sickness had left Ned Kern unable to walk; it had also greatly weakened Frémont, leaving him alternately indecisive and recklessly impulsive.

With the party on the verge of panic, in late December Frémont dispatched its four strongest members—Williams, Frederick Creutzfeldt, Thomas Breckenridge, and Henry King, an experienced traveler who had been with Frémont on two other expeditions—to walk toward Taos, some 160 miles distant, in search of help. He planned to lead the rest of the party southwest to the headwaters of the Rio Grande, where they could rest and wait for the rescue party to return, but the 15-mile journey took the weakened main body of the expedition 20 days to complete. During its course, the last mule was eaten, and Raphael Proue, a rugged French voyageur, screamed that his legs were frozen, laid down in the snow, and died.

This first casualty stunned Frémont, who suddenly seemed to recognize the desperation of his situation. With no help apparently forthcoming from the rescue party, he announced that he and four others—Godey and his nephew Theodore, Charles Preuss, and Saunders Jackson, a former slave who served as the Pathfinder's personal servant—would themselves set out in search of assistance. They took with them half of the remaining provisions, which were meager indeed, leaving the remainder for the other men of the party. According to Mijah McGehee, a

Frederic Remington's Frémont's Retreat from the San Luis Valley. *Once the horses and mules were exhausted as a source of food, some of the unfortunate members of the expedition resorted to cannibalism in order to keep themselves alive.*

member of the expedition, Frémont also left behind him written parting instructions "which we scarcely knew how to interpret." The Pathfinder ordered the famished and frostbitten party to "finish packing the baggage and hasten down as speedily as possible to the mouth of the Rabbit River where we would meet relief and that if we wished to see him we must be in a hurry about it, as he was going on to California."

From that point, the expedition disintegrated. The group left behind in the mountains was forced to survive on boiled rawhide and rope, wax candles, and boot leather. They attempted to follow Frémont's orders, but individuals continued to sicken and die. Others grew crazed and simply wandered off on their own. In the San Luis Valley, about halfway to Taos, Frémont's party came upon the earlier rescue group around the embers of a dying campfire. Although frostbitten and skeletal, Creutzfeldt, Williams, and Breckenridge still clung to life. King was not so fortunate. Frémont found his body at another campsite 200 yards away; it was obvious that after his death his comrades had fed on his remains in order to keep themselves alive.

Remington's portrayal of Bill Williams, Frederick Creutzfeldt, Thomas Breckenridge, and Henry King—the four men sent by Frémont to walk out of the mountains for help—keeping cold vigil around a campfire illustrated Breckenridge's 1896 account of the expedition.

While Frémont's band continued on to Taos, the party in the mountains descended into chaos. Most semblance of order vanished, and it was essentially each man for himself. The party split into several small groups; the stronger preyed on the weaker, stealing food, weapons, and even clothing. More men died—of the cold, of hunger, of exhaustion, or of a combination of the three.

Frémont and Godey reached Taos in late January. (As the strongest of their party, they had ridden ahead.) They stumbled into a trading post there, where they encountered Kit Carson and Lucien Maxwell. While Frémont recuperated at Carson's home, where he assured Jessie by letter "that the survey has been uninterrupted up to this point and I shall carry it on consecutively," Godey immediately set out back into the terrible mountains, this time at the head of a rescue party. By February 11, he had completed a heroic 320-mile round trip over unforgiving terrain and succeeded in rounding up all of the survivors and getting them to safety.

In all 10 men had died, but Frémont seemed remarkably undisturbed by the catastrophe. He shrugged off the recriminations of Kern and other members of the party, putting the blame all on Williams, who, Frémont said, clearly knew less about the high country than he said he did. Nor did Frémont view the expedition as in any way a failure: "The result was entirely satisfactory. It convinced me that neither snow of winter nor mountain ranges were obstacles in the way of a [rail]road." After a sufficient period of recovery in Taos, Frémont assembled the survivors of the disaster who were still willing to travel with him, along with some new recruits, and rode off to California, along a trail far south of the desolate mountains. Williams was among those who remained behind. In the spring he led an expedition back into the San Juan Mountains to recover whatever equipment had been left behind, but neither he nor any of his men were ever heard from again.

The heroic Alexis Godey helped get Frémont to safety in Taos, then headed back into the mountains and succeeded in rescuing the other survivors.

The Final Journey

As Frémont had intimated in his letter to Benton, his days as an explorer were drawing to an end, but the same could not be said of his days as a public figure. Gold strikes on Las Mariposas made him a fabulously wealthy man—29 separate veins of gold were found on his property—and in California, if not in Washington, he was still regarded as a national hero, albeit as much for his role in helping California achieve its independence as for the contributions his exploration had made to science and geography. Accordingly, as California readied itself for statehood in 1849, Frémont was asked to stand for election as one of the state's two senators. Although in some quarters his unyielding opposition to the expansion of slavery—a position he shared with his father-in-law—made him anathema, he still won election. In January 1850, the Frémonts set off for Washington, with Jessie greatly anticipating their triumphant return to the city where they had been disgraced less than three years earlier.

Because of the timing of California's entry into the union, Frémont's term in the Senate lasted just 21 days, but he made the most of them. He introduced 18 separate pieces of legislation, including several concerning the establishment of a public educational system and university. The national press made as much of him as ever, and his debates on the Senate floor with slavery advocates were widely followed, particularly his confrontations with Senator Henry Stuart Foote of Mississippi. When Foote, a notorious toper, one day drunkenly accused Frémont of

This photograph of John Frémont with Jessie was probably taken in the 1880s.

As secretary of war under James Buchanan, Jefferson Davis refused to give Frémont command of an exploring expedition. Davis went on to serve as president of the Confederacy during the Civil War.

proposing mining legislation for his own enrichment, Frémont challenged him to a duel. Violence was averted, but the brouhaha was the talk of the capital.

Nevertheless, Frémont's position on the peculiar institution cost him reelection when the proslavery faction gained the upper hand in California. He was not terribly disappointed, however, for there was now money and time to do the things with his family that had never been possible while he was exploring the wilderness. Another son, John Charles, Jr., was born in April 1851, and the entire family spent much of the next year in Europe. While in London, Frémont was thrown into jail, a misunderstanding resulting from the U.S. government's refusal to honor several bills held by British creditors from the time when Frémont had acted as governor of California, but the affair's positive resolution enabled the family to look upon it as a comical interlude in an altogether enjoyable trip.

But after Frémont's return to the United States, it soon became apparent to him that he had not yet gotten the wilderness fully out of his blood. The construction of a transcontinental railroad was the new dream of the expansionists, and the government was involved in commissioning surveys of likely routes. The railroad was a project Frémont wholeheartedly supported, regarding it as the newest twist on his father-in-law's old notion of the opening of the West as the first step on the road to Asia. He wrote later:

> It seems a treason against mankind and the spirit of progress which marks the age, to refuse to put this one completing link to our national prosperity and the civilization of the world. Europe still lies between Asia and America; build this railroad and things will have revolved about; America will lie between Asia and Europe—the golden vein which runs through the history of the world will follow the iron track to San Francisco, and the Asiatic trade will finally fall into its last and permanent road.

Despite his enthusiasm, Frémont's reputation made it impossible for him to secure government backing for a new expedition. The man responsible for approving such projects, Secretary of War Jefferson Davis, was a West Point graduate suspicious of Frémont's non-academy background and notoriety for disregarding military protocol. Even worse, from Frémont's point of view, Davis was, like Foote, a Mississippian and believed that it was the inalienable right of every white American to own slaves.

Frémont had other connections, however, and Benton was once again able to put him together with some private investors looking to finance a survey of a proposed railway line. Although the Frémonts had a new baby girl, Anne Beverly, born in early 1853, to take care of, by this point Jessie was well used to the absences of her wilderness-loving husband, and his newest project did not much faze her. She had long since noticed that he only seemed relaxed when he was with his rough-hewn male colleagues, and she confided to a friend that her spouse lacked "a parental instinct." For most of their marriage, she wrote later, her husband had been "only a guest—dearly loved & honored but not counted on for worse as well as better." Although often ill, Jessie was a person of remarkable strength and courage. She had grown accustomed to relying on herself, and to a lesser extent, on her father and mother; thus, when baby Anne died in July 1853, it was Jessie who summoned the strength to carry on in the face of this latest tragedy. Wrote Frémont: "It was she who remained dry-eyed to comfort me, for I was unmanned over the cruelty of this bereavement. Her calm stoicism, so superior to mere resignation, soon shamed me into control."

Composed once more, Frémont set out from Westport at the head of his expedition in late October 1854. Remarkably, he intended once again to make a winter crossing of the San Juan Mountains, this time by a more

The bushy-bearded Solomon Nunes Carvalho was hired by Frémont to serve as photographer on his final expedition.

A handbill for Carvalho's Charleston studios. The public was fascinated with the new art of photography, which was one reason why Carvalho could charge the somewhat exorbitant price (for that period) of $1.50 for a sitting.

northerly route. If the purpose of the mission on which he was engaged did not indicate to Frémont that his beloved West was changing irrevocably, there were other signs. Bent's Fort was no longer in existence; its proprietor, William Bent, had blown it up a few years earlier after a yellow fever epidemic. It was unlikely that Kit Carson would ride to the party's rescue should it encounter trouble; word had it that Kit had settled down somewhat and was either farming a claim or serving as an Indian agent in Taos. If the railroad would change the face of the West, another new technology, the camera, would change the way that face was seen, and Frémont had brought a daguerreotyper along with him. (A daguerreotype was an early type of photograph.) There were fewer old friends along for this journey as well. The photographer, Solomon Carvalho, and an artist, F. W. von Egloffstein, were intended as replacements for Preuss, who had never quite recovered in body and mind from the hellish fourth expedition. After some further physical trials, the acidic cartographer hung himself in September 1854.

In the mountains, Frémont encountered the same problems as he had on his previous expedition, and starvation and frostbite were again the lot of his party. Mules and horses were slaughtered for food, and the men even boiled down a porcupine. Greater tragedy was averted only because of the comparative mildness of the winter; even so, one man died, and at one point even Frémont's will gave out and he sat on the snowy trail to wait for death to take him. But he soon regained his strength, and in February 1854 the emaciated band of explorers staggered into the Mormon settlement of Parowan, in present-day southwestern Utah. After a couple of weeks of recovery, Frémont and a few others struck out southwest across the Great Basin. By springtime he was in San Francisco, and his days as an explorer were finally over.

Steamboats carried the Pathfinder back to Washington, where Jessie and the rest of the family were waiting in a

rented home not far from the Bentons'. With the slavery issue threatening to tear the Union apart, public interest in exploration was waning, but Frémont was still destined to play a not inconsiderable role in the political and military conflicts that would shape his nation's future.

In the 1850s, a new political group rose from the wreckage of the Whig party, which had been torn asunder by sectional differences, chiefly over slavery. The Republicans were formed as an antislavery party, although there was much room for disagreement between the party's left wing, which favored outright abolition of slavery in all of the nation's states and territories, and its more moderate members, who wished only to halt its expansion into the territories and new states. The fledgling party was in need of a nationally recognizable figure to head its ticket in the presidential campaign of 1856, and Frémont seemed the ideal choice. "The romance of his life and position" would win him votes, cooed one Republican strategist, as would his impeccable antislavery credentials and family connections as the son-in-law of Old Bullion, who had lost his seat in the Senate because of his antislavery stand.

At age 43, Frémont was the youngest presidential candidate in the nation's history, and he received a rough welcome to national party politics. No issue aroused the

Parowan, Utah, the Mormon settlement into which a badly shaken Frémont and his band of explorers staggered in February 1854. While still in the San Juan Mountains, Frémont, frightened that the journey was turning into a replica of the tragic fourth expedition, made his men swear that they would not resort to cannibalism.

The celebrated lithographer Nathaniel Currier was hired by the Republican party to produce this poster for Frémont's 1856 presidential campaign. William L. Dayton, a former senator from New Jersey, was Frémont's running mate.

passions as did slavery, and the Democrats did not hesitate to resort to race baiting. They warned fearful whites that the "one aim of the party that supports Frémont" was "to elevate the African race in this country to complete equality of political and economic condition with the white man" and perverted the Republican slogan of Free Soil, Free Speech, Free Men, and Frémont to Free-Soilers, Frémonters, Free Niggers, and Freebooters. While Republican supporters issued adoring campaign biographies (the famous poet John Greenleaf Whittier even glorified Frémont in a poem, *The Pass of the Sierras*, for the campaign), Democrats attacked his lineage, his religion, and his career. He was scorned as a bastard, accused of being a Catholic (at the time, the United States was an overwhelmingly Protestant society, and Catholics, many of whom were immigrants and were viewed as being un-American, were the object of virulent prejudice; although his father had been Catholic, Frémont was a Presbyterian), and criticized for the disasters in the mountains and his court-martial. The veracity of his accounts of his wilderness adventures were called into question, as was his competence in the wild, and he was painted as a vainglorious, pompous fool. It was charged that he had falsely claimed to be the discoverer of South Pass and that Jessie had actually written his books, and Democrats and Know-Nothings began to use the nickname Pathfinder in a sneering, sarcastic fashion. (Know-Nothings were members of the American party, another offshoot of the Whigs. Its members were pledged to vote only for native-born Protestants for political office; when asked about their organization and its aims, members were supposed to reply, "I know nothing." The American party's nominee in the 1856 election was former president Millard Fillmore.)

Realizing that he was not well suited for speechifying, Frémont let the energy of his supporters fuel the campaign. The Republicans held huge torchlit rallies at which special campaign songs were sung. The poet Henry Wadsworth

Longfellow, a Republican, confessed that he "found it difficult to sit still with so much excitement in the air." Battle lines were being drawn for the election that would split the country in half just four years later, and voter interest in the election was intense. Southern states threatened to secede from the Union if Frémont was elected, and the results on election day confirmed, if such confirmation was needed, that the country was divided, seemingly irrevocably, on sectional lines that reflected each region's stand on slavery. The upper northern states—New England, Michigan, Wisconsin, as well as New York, Ohio, and Iowa—went overwhelmingly for Frémont and the antislavery platform. (A remarkable 83 percent of the electorate in the North cast a ballot on election day.) He received nearly 60 percent of the popular vote there, but nearly all the remaining states, 19 in all, went to the Democratic candidate, James Buchanan. (Maryland supported the Know-Nothings.)

The election loss seemed to mark the beginning of a long dark period in Frémont's life. In 1858, his patron,

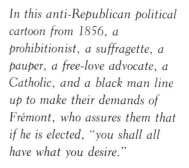

In this anti-Republican political cartoon from 1856, a prohibitionist, a suffragette, a pauper, a free-love advocate, a Catholic, and a black man line up to make their demands of Frémont, who assures them that if he is elected, "you shall all have what you desire."

friend, and father-in-law, Thomas Hart Benton, passed away. Three years later, with the outbreak of the Civil War, Frémont received a commission in the Union army as a major general from President Abraham Lincoln and was given command over the entire Department of the West, which consisted mainly of Missouri.

The command seemed a prime opportunity, but it required a politician as well as a soldier, and Frémont had demonstrated that he was temperamentally unsuited to be either. Missouri was a slave state that had chosen to remain in the Union, at least for the time being; retaining Missouri, as well as Kentucky, Delaware, and Maryland, also slave states loyal to the Union, was a cornerstone of Lincoln's early war strategy. Within Missouri's borders raged a microcosm of the greater conflict that was rending the nation, as Confederate troops and pro-Confederacy guerrilla forces battled the Union forces. As a struggle for the support of the state's populace was also being fought, the position of commander of the Department of the West required a sensitivity to public opinion as well as a grasp of military tactics.

Frémont possessed neither. Lincoln wished little from him other than that he secure Missouri for the Union, but Frémont instead spent much of his time conceiving a plan for a massive offensive down the length of the Mississippi River. In the meantime, his troops were mauled twice in the early days of the war by Confederate forces, at Wilson's Creek and at Springfield. The defeats sent shock waves through the Union high command, which was already reeling from the Union loss at the Battle of Bull Run.

Frémont then compounded his difficulties by assuming all of "the administrative powers of the state," declaring martial law, and announcing that all captured Confederate guerrillas would be executed, that the property of all pro-Confederate activists would be confiscated, and that all their slaves would be freed. This last declaration stunned

Lincoln. At this point, the North's stated purpose in fighting the war was to preserve the Union, not to abolish slavery; news that the Union intended to free the slaves was certain to drive the swing states into the Confederate camp. Lincoln advised Frémont as much and asked him to rescind his emancipation proclamation. A more politically astute or less cocksure individual would have treated the president's request as tantamount to an order, but Frémont did not. Instead, he sent Jessie to Washington to convince the president that her husband knew better than he did. On the day after her visit, Lincoln ordered Frémont to rescind his declaration (he also forbade Frémont to execute prisoners); several days later he relieved the Pathfinder of his command.

Frémont's actions did endear him to the abolitionist wing of the Republican party, and under intense political pressure, Lincoln was forced to give him a chance to redeem himself. In 1862 he was appointed commander of the newly created Department of West Virginia, with orders to prepare his 33,000 troops there for an assault against Knoxville, Tennessee, some 250 miles to the south. But the Confederate forces in the Shenandoah Valley region, under the command of Thomas "Stonewall" Jackson, had other ideas. With their dour commander driving them relentlessly, Jackson's forces proved themselves remarkably mobile; although they numbered only half as many as their opponents, they defeated the Union forces in five consecutive battles in the valley. Jackson's unpredictability and mastery of guerrilla tactics kept the Union forces constantly off guard, and in each battle he was able to bring more soldiers to the field than his Union counterpart. To Frémont and the other bedeviled Union generals, Jackson seemed a demonic spirit, able to conjure up himself and his troops out of thin air wherever they could do the most damage. Jackson's Shenandoah campaign is still regarded by military historians as a masterpiece. When a displeased Lincoln placed Frémont's command under the supervision

Frémont as a major general in the Union army. The sword he is holding was made by Tiffany's and was a special gift to him from the men who had served under him on his western expeditions.

of another general, John Pope, Frémont asked to be relieved.

He sat out the rest of the war in New York City. Las Mariposas had slowly been slipping from his grip; the estate was what was known as a floating claim, meaning that its legal title could not be clearly established. When in the frenzy of the California gold fever of the 1850s, claims jumpers had begun working and settling parts of Frémont's acreage, he had had little legal recourse. Simply maintaining the huge ranch had eaten away at his capital, and when Frémont found himself overburdened with other business interests, he simply took out further mortgages on his land. Ultimately, he was forced to sell. During the Civil War the Frémonts also lost their other California property, 12 acres opposite Alcatraz that they called Black Point, when the Union army, deeming the spot strategically desirable, seized the land and constructed a garrison, Fort Mason, there.

His other business interests enabled Frémont and Jessie to live in grand style for a while. They maintained an elegant brownstone on West 19th Street in New York City and an estate of more than 100 acres farther up the Hudson River, just north of Tarrytown, New York, but when the Memphis & El Paso Railroad, into which Frémont had sunk most of his remaining cash, went belly up in the

The bloodied and beaten forces of Frémont's armies retreat up the Shenandoah Valley. Stonewall Jackson consistently outwitted and outmaneuvered Frémont and the other Union commanders in the valley.

financial panic of 1873, the Frémont fortune also collapsed. The remainder of his days were spent in genteel poverty, eased only by a temporary appointment as territorial governor of Arizona from 1878 to 1883 and what income Jessie was able to generate as a writer from the sale of memoirs and articles. The Frémonts were forced to move around quite a bit, to California and Arizona and then back east. The now white-haired Pathfinder spent a good portion of the 1880s composing his memoirs, hoping to duplicate the extraordinary success that another great American hero, Ulysses S. Grant, had enjoyed with his autobiography, but when the first volume of Frémont's *Memoirs of My Life*, which recounted his adventures through the third expedition, appeared in 1887, it met with an indifferent public and critical response. In 1890, after lobbying by some of Frémont's old friends, Congress voted to restore him to the rank of major general and give him the pension accruing to an officer of that rank.

In July of that year, while Frémont was visiting New York City, he became very ill. Peritonitis set in, most likely from a ruptured appendix or a severe ulcer. On July 13, in a hotel room in midtown, he died. Frémont was buried across the Hudson River from Tarrytown, in the town of Piermont, whose village trustees had asked that they be allowed to honor the Pathfinder by donating a grave site and erecting a monument. At the time of his death, the population of California, the state whose name Frémont whispered with his dying breath, had increased more than fiftyfold from the time when Frémont helped wrest it from Mexico. Three days before his death, Wyoming had become the 44th state; Utah would follow six years later. From the other western territories Frémont had explored had already been carved the states of Minnesota, North and South Dakota, Nebraska, Kansas, Colorado, Nevada, Oregon, Washington, and Idaho, demonstrating the figurative truth of Jessie's assertion that "cities have risen on the ashes of his lonely campfires."

The Pathfinder in later life. A controversial public figure, he inspired great loyalty in most of those who knew him. His scientific and surveying work was crucial in opening America beyond the Mississippi, and his heroic image and legend helped imbue the West with the romance with which it is still colored. He remains a symbol of a younger, untamed, and adventurous America.

Further Reading

Bidwell, John. *Echoes of the Past: An Account of the First Emigrant Trains to California, Frémont in the Conquest of California, the Discovery of Gold & Early Reminiscences.* 1914. Reprint. Salem, NH: Ayer, 1973.

Bushford, Herbert, and Han Wagner. *A Man Unafraid: The Story of John Charles Frémont.* San Francisco: Han Wagner, 1927.

Cline, Gloria Griffen. *Exploring the Great Basin.* Norman: University of Oklahoma Press, 1963.

Dellenbaugh, Frederick S. *Frémont and '49.* New York: Putnam, 1914.

Egan, Ferol. *Frémont: Explorer for a Restless Nation.* Garden City, NY: Doubleday, 1977.

Eyre, Alice. *The Famous Frémonts and Their America.* Boston: The Christopher Publishing House, 1961.

Frémont, John C. *Memoirs of My Life.* New York: Belford, Clarke, 1887.

Gilbert, Bil. *The Trailblazers.* Alexandria, VA: Time-Life Books, 1973.

Goetzmann, William H. *Army Exploration in the American West: 1803–63.* New Haven: Yale University Press, 1959.

————. *Exploration and Empire: The Explorer and the Scientist in the Winning of the American West.* New York: Norton, 1966.

————. *Exploring the American West: 1803–79.* Handbook 116. Washington, DC: National Park Service, 1982.

———. *New Lands, New Men*. New York: Viking, 1986.

Gudde, Erwin G., and Elizabeth K. Gudde, eds. *Exploring with Frémont: The Private Diaries of Charles Preuss*. Norman: University of Oklahoma Press, 1958.

Guild, Thelma S., and Harvey L. Carter. *Kit Carson: A Pattern for Heroes*. Lincoln: University of Nebraska Press, 1984.

Herr, Pamela. *Jessie Benton Frémont*. New York: Watts, 1987.

Jackson, Donald, and Mary Lee Spence. *The Expeditions of John Charles Frémont*. Vols. 1–3. Chicago: University of Illinois Press, 1970.

McPherson, James M. *Battle Cry of Freedom*. New York: Oxford University Press, 1988.

Morrison, Dorothy Nafus. *Under a Strong Wind: The Adventures of Jessie Benton Frémont*. New York: Atheneum, 1983.

Nevins, Allan. *Frémont: Pathmarker of the West*. New York: Ungar, 1955.

Parkman, Francis, Jr. *The Oregon Trail*. 1849. Reprint. New York: Penguin, 1985.

Viola, Herman J. *Exploring the West*. Washington, DC: Smithsonian Books, 1987.

Viola, Herman J., and Carolyn Margolis, eds. *Magnificent Voyagers: The U.S. Exploring Expedition, 1838–42*. Washington, DC: Smithsonian Books, 1985.

Chronology

Entries in roman type refer to events directly related to exploration and Frémont's life; entries in italics refer to important historical and cultural events of the era.

1804   Lewis and Clark expedition begins

1813   Born John Charles Frémon in Savannah, Georgia, to Anne Pryor and Jean Charles Frémon

1821   *Missouri Compromise allows Missouri and Maine to enter the Union*

1823   *Monroe Doctrine closes American continent to colonial settlements by European powers*

1833   Frémont serves as a math teacher on the warship *Natchez* during its tour of the coast of South America; *Davy Crockett's autobiography is best-seller*

1835   Frémont begins first expedition with Captain William G. Williams; *Texas declares its right to secede from Mexico*

1836   Frémont embarks on second expedition with Williams, this time to survey the Cherokee Territory

1838   Helps survey the northern territory of the Mississippi Valley under the command of Joseph Nicolas Nicollet

1839   Goes on second expedition with Nicollet; *first baseball game is played, at Cooperstown, New York*

1840s   *1.6 million European immigrants enter the United States*

1841   Frémont elopes with Jessie Benton

1842   Leads his first expedition to explore the Oregon Trail; scales Frémont Peak

1843   Begins his second expedition, which at its conclusion marks the most complete reconnaissance of the West to date

1844   *Samuel Morse's telegraph is used for the first time between Baltimore and Washington*

1845   *Zachary Taylor moves American troops to Rio Grande*; Senate publishes Frémont's record of the second expedition; Frémont begins third expedition

1847   Embroils himself in the Bear Flag Rebellion, is appointed governor of California, and is arrested by General Stephen Kearny for mutiny; *gold discovered in California*

1848   Frémont resigns from U.S. Army; begins his fourth expedition, in the course of which 10 men are killed

1850   *California is admitted to the Union as a free state*; Frémont is elected U.S. senator from California; *Nathaniel Hawthorne's* The Scarlet Letter *is published*

1851   *Herman Melville's* Moby Dick *is published*

1853   Frémont begins his fifth expedition; *Samuel Colt introduces the mass production of small firearms*

1854   *Congress passes the Kansas-Nebraska Act*

1856   Frémont is nominated for president by the Republican party but loses election to James Buchanan

1859   *Oregon becomes the 33rd state*

1860   *Abraham Lincoln is elected 16th president of the United States*

1861   *Civil War begins*; Lincoln appoints Frémont major general; he is relieved of duty by Lincoln after issuing premature "emancipation proclamation"

1865   *Civil War ends; Lincoln assassinated*

1870   Frémont loses his fortune after Memphis & El Paso Railroad goes bankrupt

1876   *General George Armstrong Custer and all his troops are killed by Sioux and Cheyenne warriors at the Battle of the Little Bighorn*

1878   Frémont is appointed governor of the Arizona Territory

1884   *Mark Twain's* The Adventures of Huckleberry Finn *is published*

1887   Frémont publishes *Memoirs of My Life*

1890   Dies in New York City of peritonitis

Index

Picture Credits

Edward D. Harris is a teaching assistant at the University of Texas at Austin, where he is completing a dissertation in Western American history as part of his work for his Ph.D. He received a B.A. from Yale University in 1984 and taught history at a private secondary school for three years.

William H. Goetzmann holds the Jack S. Blanton, Sr., Chair in History at the University of Texas at Austin, where he has taught for many years. The author of numerous works on American history and exploration, he won the 1967 Pulitzer and Parkman prizes for his *Exploration and Empire: The Role of the Explorer and Scientist in the Winning of the American West, 1800–1900*. With his son William N. Goetzmann, he coauthored *The West of the Imagination*, which received the Carr P. Collins Award in 1986 from the Texas Institute of Letters. His documentary television series of the same name received a blue ribbon in the history category at the American Film and Video Festival held in New York City in 1987. A recent work, *New Lands, New Men: America and the Second Great Age of Discovery*, was published in 1986 to much critical acclaim.

Michael Collins served as command module pilot on the *Apollo 11* space mission, which landed his colleagues Neil Armstrong and Buzz Aldrin on the moon. A graduate of the United States Military Academy, Collins was named an astronaut in 1963. In 1966 he piloted the *Gemini 10* mission, during which he became the third American to walk in space. The author of several books on space exploration, Collins was director of the Smithsonian Institution's National Air and Space Museum from 1971 to 1978 and is a recipient of the Presidential Medal of Freedom.

DATE DUE